My Priva

with

Van Cliburn

By

Christine Rakela

Christine Rakela

NYPUBLISHERS

445 Broad Hollow Road

Melville, NY 11747

Printed in the United States of America

For a selection of the author's books please visit:
www.christinerakela.com

Disclaimer

The stories portrayed in this book reflect the author's memories of the events of people mentioned. Some names and identifiable characteristics have been changed to protect the privacy of those depicted. Dialogue has been created from memory and facts. Since this is an account of history, historical figures are mentioned.

The cover photo of this book courtesy of The Cliburn.

Dedication

There are those who seek grandeur and few who speak with their soul, to the one man who changed the world through his spiritual essence and the true enlightenment of classical music – Van Cliburn.

Acknowledgment

First and foremost, I would like to thank God for the opportunity to write this book about my dear friend and legendary pianist, Van Cliburn.

Second, I am grateful to all the people who have supported me in writing about my relationship with Van Cliburn. I would like to thank my family and close friends for their support and encouragement, and my daughter for her inspiration.

Thirdly, I would like to thank the professional organizations and people who have given me the rights to use specific names and stories in the book.

I would also like to extend a special thank you to The Cliburn for use of photos in the book. The organization can be reached at: http://www.Cliburn.org.

Lastly, I would also like to especially thank my publisher, NY Publishers.

Christine Rakela

Table of Contents

Introduction

There was a time in history when a well-bred, young man looking for validation in the arts changed the whole world and put the United States on a pedestal. To understand how this happened, you have to go back in time to fully grasp the story and its many characters. As far back as 1934, people were still struggling to recover from the depression in 1929. A child was born in McGregor, Texas, to parents who had to wait 11 years for an offspring. Needless to say, they were thrilled. His name was Harvey Laven Cliburn Junior, otherwise known as Van Cliburn. Van experienced a modest, but proper upbringing to parents who loved him. They wanted everyone else to love him too, but that wasn't always the case as jealousy at times reared its ugly head. When others saw his talent at the Julliard School of Music, jealousy started brewing. "I remember when I did not want to play the exit recital at the Julliard in front of others. There was a sea of people - I battled it out and did very well. I did two encores, the second one was very good, so I stopped after that one."

Van realized as he was growing up that reward and fame come with a heavy price. One that he was not prepared for in his upbringing.

In late 1957, Van was practicing at the Julliard under the tutelage of Rosina Lhevinne, a gold medalist herself. He was preparing for the first Tchaikovsky Piano Competition to be held in Moscow. On the other side of the world, the Soviet Union was expecting a win for a Russian pianist, but was also preparing for victory in space. With the launch of a satellite called Sputnik 1, the Russians were ahead of the United States in the race to space. This satellite could fly around the entire globe and be viewed from Earth. The United States was suddenly taken off guard as it was the Cold War and the Soviet Union, a communist country, was succeeding. The United States unexpectedly found competition through a whole new medium - classical music! Little did anyone know the magnitude of what was about to take place. Van continued to perfect his skills and in April of 1958 was soon to show the world his true talent. To be the best, you have to play the best. Van expressed, "My mother made me play the two hardest pieces." There is no question that Russia was Van Cliburn's deciding moment. And it came at a time when the world was in turmoil. Van mentioned how he felt only warmth and appreciation from the audience while he played, but not the jury, who were the ones to decide his fate. A gold medal performance shocked the world and not only put the United States back on its proud pedestal, but dissolved the intent of the Cold War and gave the world the best prize of all - a perfect performance! Who would ever think that the beauty of classical music would bring peace? This prized performance brought out the best in everyone. A country that was struggling realized a new hero. Discovered by the Russians, but lifted up by the Americans, a new inspiration that everyone wanted to hear.

Maintaining that feat over the years brought on a whole new challenge, one that fell in my lap in 1994. A person whom I hardly knew became a dear friend who shared everything with me only because he could. I experienced the heights and the depths with Van Cliburn. For almost two decades, it was my great joy of meeting him and the tragedy of his loss.

Here is my representation of Van Cliburn in my desire to express not only a revealing, inspiring, and more meaningful side of Van Cliburn, but his true wisdom. I can only hope that in this account of Van Cliburn's life, I have served him well so the world could understand and embrace not only who he really was, but what he left for us, a monument for classical music. There are some men that lift up nations, Van Cliburn did it with ease and masterfully.

Chapter 1

The Phone Call

I n 1994, Van Cliburn had recently returned to a very familiar place - the stage. He was engaged in playing a concert at Lincoln Center in New York City when he heard his mother had a stroke and was quickly declining. Chartering a plane after the concert, he rushed to her side. Shortly thereafter, his mother, teacher, advisor, and confidant gently passed away. Van loved and greatly admired his mother. For Van credited her for being as good a pianist as he, even though she had received little recognition for her talent. This became a trying time for Van to lose the one person who totally understood him.

Although his mother was irreplaceable, Van needed someone to help guide him through what seemed to be a cloudy maze. He gradually started looking for someone to fill her shoes. Van not only wanted to speak to someone who could advise him as his mother did for his career, but someone with whom he could share his thoughts and feelings, someone he could trust. Reaching out to two of his friends, who also happened to be clients of mine, Van acquired my phone number. They felt I might have the expertise to offer Van Cliburn advice at this important juncture in his life.

I was in Danville, California, spending time with my family, when one afternoon on my private number, the phone rang, and I will never forget his opening line as I answered the phone, "Christine! Well, hello! This is Van Cliburn." His signature greeting I would hear for almost twenty years. His was a voice that inspired the depths of my soul - that lifted one's spirit to pursue more from life. Such was the beginning of a private relationship that guided Van Cliburn through the next two decades of his legendary life. What I was to encounter would open up my mind to a world I would have never known.

Chapter 2

Guiding Van Cliburn

As we became better acquainted, I started to gain a solid position in Van Cliburn's life. Being Van's advisor, confidant, and astrologer, I was privy to all of his many, many stories. He thoroughly enjoyed speaking and would go on and on about memories of his early years, playing at the Julliard, winning the gold medal in Moscow, playing with the most accomplished conductors, traveling the world, his personal life, and everything that concerned his social life, which was always abundant.

Most people don't realize the intricacies involved in guiding Van Cliburn. Besides advising him, we would enjoy the art of astrology to enhance our sessions and offer objective insight into the many personal as well as global situations that required special guidance. Fortunately, Van was educated in the world of astrology, which made our sessions that much more intriguing. In our late-night sessions, I would advise him on what he would be experiencing and how to work with the energy to improve his performance on stage or other social or personal interactions going on in his life. The amazing part was that Van was able to take the information I was giving him and apply it in that moment, oftentimes while he was performing. Pure brilliance! In our sessions, our minds worked in a similar fashion on a very intricate level that is hard to describe.

I was the only person Van could really talk to in such an open manner. Even those he was very close with did not always know what was truly on Van's mind. Van would tell me this often saying, "You don't understand what it's like to be in my position. I can't really talk to anyone, but you." I always felt honored, but I also understood why he would be saying this as his high position in the world had to be guarded. Only a select few did he honestly trust.

Our midnight working rendezvous' left me exhausted yet fulfilled. I gave Van every ounce of my mind, body, and soul when I worked for him. Listening intensely, and vigorously scurrying through the astrology charts, trying to find the most optimal days and times, I worked like a female warrior on a mission. Only my mission involved the exaltation of leading one man to enlighten the world. To say the least, it was an overwhelming responsibility, one that most people could not handle, but aside from the pressure, I loved it!

Chapter 3

The Gold Medal

T hrough our many sessions, I would soon learn about the most exciting, pivotal time in Van's life. It all started in the late spring of 1958. Van Cliburn had arrived in the capital of Russia. He was twenty-three years old. I was only three years old, growing up in a small traditional town in Northern California, certainly unaware of the historic event about to take place in Moscow. Little did I know how Van Cliburn's grand achievement would be a major part of my destiny in life and I his. Looking back, it was as if the script was already written, and all we had to do was make that one connection that would last through the years. Fortunately, it happened. Now, I can describe to you not only his real-life story, what Van actually told me, but also our fascinating journey together.

On the first day of the Tchaikovsky Piano Competition Van was scheduled to perform in, Van was instructed to choose a number that would determine when he would compete. At the time, he did not realize how this number would also mirror his destiny.

There is something to be said about the energy of numbers, for on that day, Van Cliburn picked a number that would reflect his success while playing at the first

Tchaikovsky Competition in Moscow. "I picked number fifteen," he told me. I smiled, knowing what an influence this would have had. We went on to discuss the significance of number fifteen and how it would have helped catapult him into the limelight as he would be well-taken care of and things would go his way. Without question, they certainly did!

Prior to his trip to Moscow, Van had carefully selected two of the hardest pieces to play for the competition with the encouragement of his mother. She was convinced that the most difficult piano pieces must be played, Tchaikovsky's Piano Concerto No.1 and Rachmaninoff's Piano Concerto No.3 in D minor. Rachmaninoff was a creative genius whom Van highly admired, and we would discuss his accomplished life several times over the years.

You would have never known how nervous he was with his brilliant execution of both classical compositions. Rachmaninoff's Concerto No.3 in D Minor is such a difficult piece of music that it is said that one could go insane from just playing this extremely complicated masterpiece. Van Cliburn was in complete control throughout the entire piece. Tchaikovsky's Piano Concerto No.1 is also intensely arduous and incredibly engaging. Both pieces are mentally, physically, and spiritually demanding. One's whole being must merge with the music. Van knew just how to become one with the classical music he was playing, and the results say it all.

Van told me that he was completely taken by surprise at how well-received he was by the Russian people. They literally embraced him, and their admiration showered him across the stage with an array of beautiful flowers strewn about and precious jewels littering a sparkling podium. The Russians were in absolute awe of Van Cliburn!

In fact, after performing for the rivaled competition, two of the hardest pieces ever composed, some music lovers in the ecstatic audience could not contain themselves and started chanting in Russian, "First prize! first prize!" Since the judges had previously selected a Russian pianist to be the winner, they had quite a dilemma on their hands. It was said that a few of the judges even manipulated their scores to make Van Cliburn look undeserving of the prestigious title. Other judges caught wind of what was happening and made sure their scores reflected his performance - perfect, which is what they had actually thought, perfect!

Because of all of the fanfare, the Russian government had to confront this amazing upset, as the judges had to ask permission to proceed with the award. Van told me that Nikita Khrushchev, the leader of the Soviet Union at the time, had difficulty believing that an American had won, but that it was not only the judges, but his daughter who convinced him to give Mr. Cliburn what he so deservingly earned - the gold medal!

Van had a feeling of winning, and while standing in line in the cafeteria where the competition was being held, he suddenly heard his name announced and that he had surprisingly won! No one in the Soviet Union was expecting such a winner. Someone on the microphone, too excited about the news, slipped not waiting for a formal announcement. Van thought it might be true, but was concerned at how the announcement came over a loudspeaker unexpectedly, and he just happened to hear it.

Calming Van's anxiousness, a couple of hours later, it was officially announced in the Moscow Music Hall who had won - Van Cliburn! He was greeted by an elated audience and received the prestigious gold medal. A standing ovation would ensue that almost replicated the incredibly astonishing eight-minute acknowledgement he had received after performing for the Tchaikovsky Competition! This would be the first of many standing ovations in Russia as well as throughout the world. However, there was much more to the pressure of being a worldly, celebrated classical musician.

After winning the prestigious gold medal at the first Tchaikovsky Competition, Khrushchev finally congratulated Mr. Cliburn and jokingly asked him why he was so tall. Van humorously replied, "Because I am from Texas!" This was also Van Cliburn's opportunity to see if a special request would be granted, and he asked Khrushchev if he could take a shaving of lavender off of the gravesite of Tchaikovsky. His request was approved, and somehow Van managed to bring it back to the United States, get it through customs, and plant the shaving of lavender at his home of many years in Fort Worth, where it still exists.

Chapter 4

The Secret Prediction

Although Van and I had not met, he was very aware of the possibility of winning the gold medal - it was predicted! Early on in his career, while living in New York City and attending the prestigious Julliard School, Van heard of a well-known psychic and decided to pay her a visit.

During the session, she surprisingly announced that she saw him surrounded by confetti and then point-blank told Van he would win a gold medal! Van knew that he was good enough to win, but wasn't sure when it would happen, so hearing this news was confirming his own thoughts. In the future, Van would learn to trust his intuition more. Although it was great news, he put the news aside and focused on being the best. The future would decide on his anticipated win.

Yes, on April 4, 1958, Van Cliburn won the gold medal at the first Tchaikovsky Competition in Moscow and, on his return to the United States, was given a celebrated ticker-tape parade in New York City and was showered with confetti, just as it had been predicted! Van mentioned to me that Lena Horn, a very good friend of Van's, said, "We all knew he would win. It was just a matter of time."

Chapter 5

Music in Moscow

V an would play on several occasions in Moscow and Saint Petersburg. He was welcomed by the Russian President as well. Van used to joke with him saying, "I wouldn't know a state secret if I were standing next to it." Although Van was more than capable of knowing, he was encouraged by his parents not to discuss politics. It was good advice and kept the emphasis where it should be, on the music. "I never spoke a word about politics," he would say. "They thought I was a boy from the backwoods!" We laughed!

"When Russia awarded me with the gold medal in 1958, there were so many gifts. Women would throw their jewels or anything they could onto the stage when I performed! First prize was twenty-five thousand rubles." Van gave New York City, which honored him with a ticker-tape parade, twelve thousand five hundred rubles, half of his prize money. The news described how Van Cliburn was here in New York City several times, but he thrived in this most victorious moment. Yet, there was so much more to endure. Some rewarding times, and some unforeseen times lay ahead.

Chapter 6

The Genius Within

V an's genius was discovered by his mother, and gradually, those closest to him became aware of it. I, too, was enlightened by his brilliance. The more sessions I had with Van, the more I became aware of just how intricate his mind was. He seemed to be memorizing everything I was saying and then would watch it play out and tell me about what had occurred later. I had my computer to constantly refer to, but Van was using his mind like one. I was amazed by his intelligence and appreciated how he would converse with me so easily, which enhanced an already wonderful rapport between us.

After Van Cliburn performed at the first Tchaikovsky Competition in 1958, the selected judges saw his absolute genius talent as well. Van was a pure reflection of the music, which described, on a personal note, who Van really was. Dmitri Shostakovich, chairman of the Tchaikovsky Competition, was convinced that Van Cliburn's performance was perfect!

One is always inclined to aim for perfection with your art, but when you have succeeded in becoming perfection, it is a glorious moment as the genius within is released for all to bear witness. Van Cliburn's musical genius would soon be appreciated by an unsuspecting community.

Chapter 7

Closet Christians

It was an emotional homecoming when Van Cliburn's travels led him back to Russia. Van was very aware that Russia, the Soviet Union until 1991, was not a free country. And in any communist country, those who are religious or spiritual go underground. Van gradually became aware of the closet Christians. Van was, in every respect, a Christian. The Russian Christians confided in him, saying that every time they held their meetings and times of prayer, they would play the music of Van Cliburn to secretly block out their prayers and not be discovered. They knew that everyone in the Soviet Union at this time revered Van Cliburn's music, so it was the perfect alibi! And is to this day.

Still, in an intensely communist nation, being a Christian was risking your life. During the cold war years in the communist Soviet Union, you could be prosecuted and imprisoned for expressing your religious beliefs in God.

It was a frightening time in Russia, and Van Cliburn swept the people off their feet with what Russians could embrace - classical music, which permeated their lives.

Even in prayer, he captured their hearts and gave them hope in their quest. Van was deeply moved.

These real-life stories only reinforced his powerful connection to the Russian people over the years to come. Van expressed many times to me, that although a proud Texan, he always felt that he was Russian. His deeply emotional connection with Russia was discussed often. Van loved the Russian people and was convinced he had had a past life there. To Van, it was a magical place where everything seemed to feel so familiar.

Chapter 8

Transitions in Life

B ack home, Van would confront some difficult transitions in his life that one cannot prepare for. "My father was born on December 3, 1898, in the morning. A week before he died, my father greeted me saying," "Hello sonny-boy, I love you. Look after your mother." Van Cliburn's beloved father passed away in 1978. While they were clearing out the garage in Kilgore, Texas, where Van grew up since the age of six, Van and his mother found all of these detailed, work records. "Father was an executive with Exxon Mobil and wrote up oil reports." To honor his dad, Van supported the East Texas Oil Museum in Kilgore. As a classical pianist, Van Cliburn is considered a "favorite son" of Kilgore. In a speech Van gave shortly thereafter, he said, "I was in between two pillars, classical piano and classical petroleum!" How appropriate.

As a child, Van spent much time traveling to the oil fields with his father, and at one point, he told others that his home was on Highway 259! It was on December 28, 1930, during the depression, that Lou Della Crim No. 1 well burst with oil in Kilgore. Van would be born three and a half years later. Eventually, over 1000 oil derricks were pumping oil, making this the richest acre in the world at that time. The sight of oil derricks everywhere became a normal landscape for Van Cliburn. However, he would not end up following in his father's footsteps as destiny called.

Van greatly admired his father. His passing was an overwhelming loss, and he decided to take a sojourn from classical music that ended up lasting nine years. Van was passionate about playing the piano, but he never liked to perform. Before every performance, he became extremely nervous to the point that his stress was making him ill. He would sometimes joke and say, "I have had so many heart attacks on stage, I don't mind having another one." This was one of the reasons he had a nine-year "intermission," as he called it, with his career. The stress of performing was beyond overwhelming, and with the loss of this father, he needed time to adjust to an entirely new perspective on life. Upon his return in 1986, he was once again well-received by his audience and the critics. Still, he was concerned about pleasing his audience as he wasn't a young man any more.

1994 was another huge turning point for Van Cliburn as his mother, Rildia Bee, passed away with Van at her side. With the loss of his parents, Van faced an unfamiliar reality without their support that questioned his future.

Van loved his parents dearly. Both of his parents were instrumental in his life, and he was so grateful for their love and encouragement. His mother inspired him musically as well as spiritually, and his father inspired him mentally by encouraging him to read influential books such as Tolstoy, among many other great writers and philosophers, so he would acquire knowledge about the world. "My father was a great gentleman and a marvelous teacher. He was a stickler for chivalry." Van appreciated all of his father's many insights. He always felt such a strong connection to him, even in spirit. One night, when we had some time to discuss his father's astrology chart, we discovered even deeper astrological connections between Van and his father. Van was very pleased, for this confirmed what he had always felt - a tremendous bond.

With the lessons he learned from his chivalrous father, it was so apropos that Van Cliburn was knighted by Queen Elizabeth in England. He told me how he definitely enjoyed meeting Her Majesty. I often felt that Van Cliburn was truly a chivalry knight in his own right, as he was always a gentleman, just like his father.

Van often spoke about his parents. It was obvious that he missed them. He also would speak of how lucky he was to have had such wonderful parents. Van would always say to me that "A child needs a father and a mother." Through the years I would hear him say this line many times. Family meant everything to Van Cliburn.

His thoughts as a young boy would eventually come to pass. "Ever since I was four, I was frightfully nervous about losing my parents. I was also told that nothing continues." Van's parents tried to reassure him, always saying, "We love you, but we want others to love you. When we go, that's our privilege." They worried about their son in the spotlight. Although he was destined for a glamorous life, it comes with its burden. Van often said, "When every door opens, it is a door of responsibility."

Since Van had just started back with his career, the loss of his mother was a shocking blow. Throughout the years we talked, he would speak about her often. I could hear from the sound of his voice how much he missed her. As some have called his mother an unwanted burden or hindrance, I completely disagree. Her passing was a deep loss, one that could not be replaced.

During this year, Van had taken on an assistant who was impeccable about helping him. He was especially supportive when Van's mother passed. Van and his assistant had very complimentary energies. What one didn't have the other made up for. His assistant was very business-oriented, whereas Van was blessed with artistry. My interaction with Van's assistant was cordial, but limited. He possessed a pleasant personality, and I appreciated his punctuality. Van, however, was my main focus always.

Around this time, Van knew a couple, who just happened to be clients of mine after viewing one of my television shows in New York City. Being close to Van

Cliburn, they had mentioned their astrologer. Since Van was always fascinated with astrology, he decided it would be a good time for him to speak with one. The very next day, I received a call mentioning that I would be hearing from Van Cliburn. I was intrigued, but I really didn't know who Van Cliburn was. That was soon to change.

One sunny day in the mid-summer of 1994, a very special and fated meeting occurred between Van Cliburn and myself. From that moment, we started a partnership that lasted almost 20 years where I advised him constantly on all of his engagements, concerts, travel, dinners, speeches, etc... The list went on. Whatever came up, we discussed. Van trusted me implicitly. I was totally dedicated to supporting and advising him.

We both thoroughly enjoyed each other's company. Van's complete trust in me allowed me to work at my best. We understood each other on a level that evades description, getting along just swimmingly. Although challenging to do during our time together, I kept every session a secret, tucked away in the abyss of my mind.

For many years, although I knew how extremely important it was to be guiding Van Cliburn, as opposed to diverting the pressure, I relished every moment. It was an incredible challenge to see how far I could take my knowledge as an astrologer and advisor. Since I possessed an earned confidence in the way I conducted my sessions, I aimed at getting the most accurate results. There was no room for error.

Pursuing my own dreams kept me from becoming a worker bee. Some would not have considered me to be Van's equal, but in my mind, I always was. How else could I have been able to have the confidence to guide him? I was just in another field working behind the scenes. Being one of the few professional, certified astrologers in the country, I was at the peak of my career when Van came into my life. I always felt guiding Van was like a mission I had already signed up for before I came into this incarnation. Our chemistry indicated a seemingly faultless friendship that I thought would never end.

Chapter 9

Chemistry

I t is rare in life that you come across an incredible connection with another person. In analyzing Van Cliburn's astrology with my own, the cosmic connections between Van and me were so evident. We agreed on everything and communicated so extremely well that I sometimes wondered, if we were in another lifetime, whether we would have had a closer relationship. There was something idyllic about our midnight sessions that held a mutual interest, but I was clear about my place in his life as his adviser, which was soon to become a dear friend.

Of course, in New York City, the lights never go down unless there is an unexpected blackout. Yet, on the 20th floor on the Upper West Side, the peace and quiet, the stillness of the night, allowed Van and I to diligently focus, mulling over chart after chart, and finding those optimal times and the best path to follow with just about every life situation. I cherish those memories.

Van and I were so in sync with each other that he never seemed to call when I was sick, and he could tell when I was away. Van was much better at trusting his intuition than I. Still, on and off throughout the day, Van was on my mind, especially when playing a concert. I could visualize him playing in his stylish, dramatic, yet meaningful fashion, beautifully lifting his hand from each key as if he were sliding into an ethereal world. Van spoke of how the main point of playing well was "playing into the keys and feeling the music." He expressed how some pianists did not possess this talent. Everything was technically perfect, but there was no connection with the soul. As one needs to merge with the soul to express one's true artistry, for Van and I, it was the friendship of two souls working in harmony to release the optimal in classical music and everything it involved.

Chapter 10

Jealousy and More

W hen Van Cliburn played a concert for the first time at Carnegie Hall in New York City on May 19, 1958, he told me a good friend and wonderful opera singer, Rise Stevens, sent him flowers, wishing him good luck. He never forgot the warm gesture, as during his earlier years, there was such tremendous jealousy and envy of his incredible talent amongst his colleagues. This performance of Tchaikovsky's Piano Concerto No.1 was recorded live and not only earned him triple platinum status, but Van Cliburn won a Grammy Award for the best classical performance ever!

Unbeknownst to him, after winning the gold medal in 1958 and garnering the applause of many performances that year, many would become resentful of his success. "When I came back from Russia, I had to deal with some very hurtful moments, jealousy from my colleagues." This was a terrible shock to Van, and at times, he didn't know who he could trust.

Van became sadly aware of the reality of how some people could not appreciate another's success in life. We used to talk about how important it is to appreciate the achievements of those around you. How else could you attract that same success for yourself? He would mention this often, adding, "When you are jealous of others, it only keeps you from your own success."

Van became very cautious about who he associated with and gradually found his social circle that mostly held the superbly talented. Lena Horne told Van Cliburn one day, "You belong with us," meaning that Van needed to be in close company with those who were exceptionally talented. Otherwise, he would risk the damnation of those who were riddled with jealousy and willing to undermine him.

Chapter 11

Going Beyond the Technique

A s a performer, one must develop a skilled technique and then reach beyond it to enhance the spirit of the music. Van was fortunate to have one of the best teachers in the world to encourage his artistic development, his mother. If you have ever heard Rildia Bee play the piano, her skill and mesmerizing articulation of the keys were certainly equal to her genius son. Van thought so, too.

Since Rildia Bee was also a wonderful singer, she wisely taught Van to sing each phrase of music when first learning the piano. Thus, he developed a voice-like piano phrasing with his music. "My mother had a gorgeous singing voice. She told me that the first instrument was the human voice." He added, "When you are playing the piano, you must find a singing sound with the notes - the eye of the sound, she called it."

One special technique that was elaborated upon was gently pressing into the keys. Van wanted the piano to sing, not just echo the sound of the note. Playing into the keys to allow the sound to naturally rise as opposed to it being forced. Needless to say, Van, with his long, supple fingers and keen sensitivity to sound, was the ultimate expert.

Another special technique was how to use the pedal to allow the notes to literally resonate like a refined singer to enhance their quality. Van emphasized the use of the piano pedal to work in subtle harmony with the manipulation of each key. "If you cannot feel the music, you are not a great pianist!" Van would say.

At times, Van criticized those who rose in status, but did not possess the true talent of musical expression. Saying, "Relying on one's technique does not move the soul." For Van, moving the soul was everything!

Chapter 12

Playing the Music

The artist and his instrument need to become one to fully express one's potential. Van Cliburn would describe to me many times how the piano should be played. "The piano has to be what it is, lyrical." He described how some teachers did not have the knowledge and experience to teach. "I think certain teachers lead students down the wrong path. You can play mezzo forte, giving it an illusion. You also have to create an illusion of pianissimo, performing very softly. In order to do so, you should not use the left pedal." In theatre, whatever one's craft might be, one must create an illusion that allows the audience to be transformed as the moment becomes their newly imagined reality.

Commenting on some of the greatest pianists, Van described how, "Beethoven wrote for the piano, he understood. I have grave doubts that Mozart wrote for the piano. He was thinking of the harpsichord." On the other hand, "Chopin wrote emotion into the piece, but you need to play it clearer." Van understood the sensitivity of Chopin and how his compositions needed to be played very meticulously. He described how, "the left hand is the metronome and the right hand feels it."

Van pointed out how "Classical music is not offensive. It will never hurt your ears." Commenting further, he said, "One thing is you have to be clear in what you are playing. If you play a piece slower at a grand rhythmic pace, you will sound faster than if you play faster with a lack of clarity."

Van expressed how a winner of the Van Cliburn Competition, although very good, was playing too fast. "When you play too fast, the technique is not serving the music. It's serving the ego," he would explain.

Classical music is not about the ego. It's about lifting up the soul. In having the pleasure of speaking in depth with famed conductor Mariss Jansons and asking him if the music is overwhelming at times, he smiled and said, "There are times when the whole room opens up and all you see and feel is God!" This is no doubt what Van Cliburn felt when immersed in the music. We would talk about such times when something extraordinary was happening on stage, in the moment. It is a reward in itself to experience the deepest level possible with classical music when pure bliss becomes the music. This was always the true objective of Van Cliburn.

Chapter 13

The Art is Richer than the Prize

Van Cliburn's celebrity status would attract a very handsome fee for his artistic services, playing concerts. However, it was never about the money, but about satisfying his audience, which was his serious, ultimate goal.

On June 18, 1994, Van Cliburn returned to New Jersey to play at the Grant Park Music Festival's 60th anniversary at an outdoor gala concert for over 350,000 people, the largest audience in attendance there! He would perform his victory piece, Tchaikovsky Piano Concerto No. 1. "Tchaikovsky is the most beloved composer. His music is irresistible. You have to love it!" Van would exclaim. "Tchaikovsky is a world treasure." After a long sojourn from performing classical music, he was coaxed from semi-retirement to return to the stage. Needless to say, the audience was ecstatic!

Van Cliburn commanded a high fee with his earned prestige, but at this concert, he accepted a much smaller fee, almost equal to his earlier appearance at the park concert lawn at the start of his career. "Before I went to Russia and won the gold medal, I was paid $400 for two concerts at Grant Park for 85,000 people both nights."

Clearly, his appearance was more for the publicity. Still, and to say the least, it was impressive, especially from a man who could command an enviable fee. Van was very motivated after this performance, which was a tremendous success, and started performing more consistently throughout the world. He was pleased that, once again, he was able to inspire so many people with the joy of classical music. It was one month later, following this performance, that I met Van Cliburn through an auspicious phone call that remarkably changed both of our lives.

Chapter 14

The Piano Sings

I n getting to know Van throughout our many years I was surprised to learn of his intrigue with opera singers. Van Cliburn often expressed how he loved the opera. He would always try to get the piano to sing like an opera star! In order to achieve this sought-after goal, Van had to go beyond mastering the piano to create an illusion by manipulating the sound to "sing!" I remember him visiting New York City on several occasions to see the celebrated stars at the Metropolitan Opera House.

In November of 2004, an article came out in Opera Magazine, which included a photo of Van with opera singer Renata Tebaldi in a warm embrace. Van spoke so highly of her, saying, "She was the queen of the Met. She was fabulous. I adored her vocally, physically, and spiritually - on all levels." He exclaimed, "Renata Tebaldi was so breathtaking! She had magic that thrilled me more than playing!"

How surprising, I thought! What a powerful and enlightening statement. Through opera, Van was inspired to take his already brilliant technique to an even higher level. Since I had the pleasure of studying opera with Robert Baird, who worked with members of the

Metropolitan Opera in New York City, I could easily understand Van's appreciation for opera singing. The fact that opera singing equaled his passion for being a pianist was astounding to me! However, this was the inspiration Van needed to instill with his genius talent to enthrall the world.

Van Cliburn so admired the opera divas that when they came into town to sing, he would have them stay at his home and give them the royal treatment. I remember one invitation where he was so honored that an impressive operatic soprano was in town and made her as welcomed as possible.

Van seemed to be infatuated with all of the well-known opera singers. They all had a mesmerizing effect on him. One evening, I was watching Maria Callas on an Arts Showcase channel when Van called, and we ended up talking about Ms. Callas. He thought she was absolutely stunning! Maria Callas had her first debut at Carnegie Hall in 1959, a year after Van Cliburn made his debut. Van exclaimed, "In my opinion, opera stars are the true divas of the world."

Chapter 15

The Mathematical Equation

W hen you think of music, you don't think of a mathematical equation, but Van Cliburn did. "The highest form of music is mathematical." Van often described classical music as a mathematical equation. Possessing an incredible, genius talent for playing the piano, he would know. To play music well, one must have the mind of a mathematician. "Music inspires the mind in math," he explained. "Classical music is also spiritual, and thus it enables the soul." Van related classical music to life, saying, "Music is truth, beauty, and spirit!" Van Cliburn believed that classical music was the end- all. Without it, we were lost souls.

Van knew if he could somehow get classical music to be taken seriously in the schools in the United States, that all children would excel in math. He encouraged the musical department in Texas to include music in their curriculum. Van also donated much of his money to educate children to learn more about classical music. He felt that music changed the brainwaves in our minds, both the left and the right sides, thus balancing logic and aesthetics, which has been scientifically proven. The mind would excel to a fuller capacity of use as well as be blessed with the awareness and inspiration of classical music.

Van felt that a child is never too young to be introduced to classical music. He was convinced that for a young child to be educated, "They need to know the grand staff as well as how to read music. Knowing the three elements of music, which are melody, harmony, and rhythm, is crucial."

Van was critical of an educational system that would eliminate music and art from a child's curriculum to balance the budget. "There are so many dimensions embedded in classical music - mathematics, literature, architecture, and philosophy," Van explained. "In early BC, Plato observed that the highest form of mathematics is music!"

Chapter 16

The Van Cliburn Competition

V an Cliburn so loved classical music that in 1962, when he was approached to establish the Van Cliburn International Piano Competition in his honor, he agreed. The Van Cliburn Competition, which takes place every four years in Fort Worth, Texas, became known worldwide, and only the crème de la crème have played there. Van always knew who most likely would be the winner. Many stars were discovered at this global competition. Van was impressed with several young, talented pianists and encouraged them to further worldly status.

Although the competition represented the finest in classical piano music, behind the scenes there were the usual politics that Van had always tried to avoid. Carrying the competition was enough for him. As the years passed, he felt the need to distance himself, but still maintain a passionate involvement especially at the final event. Luckily for Van, the competition at that point was running itself. Still, it is the most respected piano competition in the world and continues to flourish.

Chapter 17

A Most Admired Composer

T he one classical musician who most inspired Van was the composer, pianist, and conductor Sergei Vasilyevich Rachmaninoff. He was one of the greatest pianists of his day and was mostly known for his romanticism in Russian classical music. Van was trained in this style. Rachmaninoff featured the piano in most of his compositions and sought out its expressive possibilities.

Van greatly admired him and always spoke so highly of his genius talent. We spent much time mulling over his astrology chart to gain added insight and try to unveil the brilliant, gifted composer that he was. Rachmaninoff was born on April 1, 1873. One of his most spectacular works was Rachmaninoff's Piano Concerto No. 3 in D Minor, a favorite of Van Cliburn's, which was performed flawlessly at the First Tchaikovsky Competition in 1958.

Van told me that when Rachmaninoff composed Concerto No. 3, "there was no note that could have gone another way." Indicating that it was perfect. Van explained that in the original recording, "Rachmaninoff did not record the 3rd very well. So I had to learn the 3rd on my own." Needless to say, Van Cliburn's interpretation of the 3rd is brilliant! Thus, winning him the ultimate prize of a gold medal in Moscow and international status. Van clearly preferred the music of Rachmaninoff, but would be introduced to a whole other side of Rachmaninoff in the future.

Chapter 18

The Sun Line – Russia

O ut of all the places in the world, when Van Cliburn was offered an engagement in Russia, he would make every effort to go. Nothing could keep him from the Russian people, whom he held close to his heart. Van felt so at home there and often discussed how he had such a strong connection that it symbolized a past life in Russia. Drawing up an astrology chart with Moscow as his birthplace clearly indicated that Van would rise to fame in the cultural megacity of Moscow.

In looking at Van's astrological influences, there was an interesting comparison. Amadeus Mozart's astrology chart and the Sun line aspecting his career sector of the chart indicate his rise to fame in Vienna, not where he was born. Mozart achieved great fame in Vienna in 1781, but was born in Salzburg, where, in his early years, he lived relatively unnoticed to the classical music world. Van was born in Shreveport, Louisiana, yet achieved great fame in Moscow.

The time of one's birth is essential when you are working with astrology. Since some astrologers had calculated Van's birth time to be twenty-five minutes later than what Van was told was his birth time, made our search for optimal times even more challenging.

For a while, there was some discrepancy about his time. However, he always remembered his father saying, "He looked at the time when his son was born, and it was 11:20 a.m., the exact time his grandmother had passed away." For an astrologer, the time of birth is the key, so we were pleased to have an exact time of birth with a real story behind it.

There were also many events that correlated to Van's chart and confirmed this time of birth. As these events occurred, I would point out the obvious connections to Van to validate what he had suspected all along. This was further confirmed when Van told me one day, "In 1986, when we were dismantling my apartment in New York City, we found my birth certificate and my mother's as well. It clearly said, 11:20 a.m." After working with several events during Van's life and rectification on his birth chart, we concluded his time of birth.

One of the key factors was Van winning the gold medal in Moscow - his sudden rise to fame. Although his peers felt he was the best, what astrologically would encourage that phenomenal event in that location?

Van's astrology chart for Moscow indicated his Cancer Sun at 19 degrees made an exact favorable aspect to the mid-heaven career cusp at 19 degrees, the top point of his birth chart in Moscow, which rules over career, reputation, acknowledgement, and status in life. Besides confirming his time of birth, the Sun in exact angle to this career point was a must in order for Van to be acknowledged by the world. This angle put his destined career in the spotlight, where it beamed brightly. So, it was fated to be in Moscow that he would rise in stature to a world-wide, recognized figure.

Chapter 19

Family Farm

B efore Van Cliburn became a household name, he had a well-mannered and modest upbringing. The family farm was in McGregor, Texas. His mother, Rildia Bee O'Bryan, was born there on October 14, 1896. She was a phenomenal pianist, but at that time, women were not encouraged to have a career, especially playing the piano, so her brilliant talent was passed on to her students and her son, Van. When he was three years of age, his mother heard Van play on the piano a tune that a student had learned earlier that day. To her surprise, she could immediately tell that Van had talent.

Once Mr. and Mrs. Cliburn realized their son was destined for a career in classical music, they moved to Kilgore when Van was six and added onto their garage a practice studio. At the age of eleven, Van went to study in New York at the Julliard school, but then turned down the opportunity, recognizing that he only wanted to study with his mother. Rildia Bee would be the chosen one to guide her gifted, genius son to glory.

Van Cliburn was born in Shreveport, Louisiana, but grew up in Kilgore, Texas. Throughout his lifetime, Van would always hear his parents say, "We wanted you.

My father, he bull-dozed into the delivery room when I was born and put the bracelet on me." A husband in the delivery room was unheard of in 1934.

Harvey Laven and Rildia Bee Cliburn tried to have a baby for eleven years, and finally, Rildia Bee became pregnant with Van. Rildia Bee went through a lot of discomfort and pain during the pregnancy as well as giving birth. Van recalled his father saying, "He would never put mother through this pain again."

In the blood type, Van was A positive, like his father, but his mother was O negative. Van thought this blood type had something to do with his mother's difficulties. At times, she felt beset with severe headaches that were excruciating. After much exploration as to why this was occurring, she was finally treated. Van felt tremendous compassion for her during these terrible bouts.

Still, Rildia Bee guided Van every step of the way to stardom. Van was excused from physical education so as not to cause injury to his hands in any way. Van told me he didn't mind. He still went to school and interacted with the other children. Somehow, he was more mature though even in his thinking, often saying to me, "I always told myself as a child, I am going to drink black coffee and smoke cigarettes." That's exactly what he did.

Chapter 20

Rildia Bee

B orn Rildia Bee O'Bryan, she was more importantly known as Van Cliburn's mother and piano teacher. "When mother was fifteen and sixteen, she was called to be a missionary, but she ended up becoming a teacher. She was always appealing to the goodness of others." Rildia Bee was a very accomplished pianist as well. She studied music at the Cincinnati Conservatory and the New York School of Musical Art, which later became the Julliard School. "Mother played two recitals, one in Laredo and the other in Shreveport."

On June 6, 1923, Rildia Bee married Harvey Laven Cliburn, an oil industry executive. "My parent's relationship was very romantic." However, "My father would have to open the door for my mother in refining my courtly duties and be so pervasive."

I was sorry I never personally knew or heard Rildia Bee's piano playing, except for a few brief moments on Van's Classical Music DVD that Van had sent to me. I felt her skills as a pianist almost surpassed even Van's. Rildia Bee studied under Arthur Friedheim, a pupil of Franz Liszt. Luckily, she was able to instill in her son the secrets of being an accomplished classical artist.

Van's love and admiration for his mother was clearly evident. Around the time of her passing in the summer of 1994, some extra stocks she owned were sold. Van decided that it wasn't his money and put all of it toward the funeral arrangements, making it a very grand event. "What was hers was hers," he said.

Van spoke of Rildia Bee often and how he missed her. He described how his mother was a very spiritual woman and inspired him to be the same. Van kept in his possession two pieces of diamond jewelry that his mother owned, and he could never part with them. As so often, people feel the energy of someone who has passed on through a piece of jewelry, Van could feel the presence of his mother.

At an auction at Christie's in New York City of several of Van's possessions, he would not give up these two diamond pieces. The psychic who predicted Van would win the gold medal in Moscow in 1958 also told him that these two diamond pieces would bring him luck. Even though they would have fetched a handsome price at the auction, Van refused to sell them and kept them close at hand because he so missed his mother's presence.

Chapter 21

57th Street

Besides Rildia Bee, Van's teachers also included Rosina Lhevinne. A gold medalist herself, she worked with Van exclusively to perfect his talent in 1951 when he was seventeen years old. Rildia Bee recommended that she be Van's instructor at the Julliard School in New York City.

Van lived on 57th Street in an apartment that accommodated his late-night practicing. The room in which he perfected his talent was sound-proofed, so when he practiced, he would not upset his neighbors. There, he would practice until 1, 2, 3, or 4 a.m.! During this time, he also established a relationship with a young woman, a soprano in the opera, that he fully appreciated since life can be very lonely, especially in New York City. His life however, revolved around playing the piano daily for hours, lost in the world of classical music.

Near his apartment on 57th street was a flower shop, whose owner Van became acquainted with over the years. He always ordered flowers from this particular flower shop and considered the owner, a proud Taurus woman, a dear friend. She had survived many difficult situations in life, and her determination was admirable.

They shared a common bond and would confide in each other often. Occasionally, I would offer advice that Van would pass along to her.

Down the street was Carnegie Hall, which first opened on May 5, 1891, by Andrew Carnegie, who wanted to do something prolific with his vast amounts of money and to secure his reputation in the future. Seven years later, after arriving in Manhattan, Van would be playing at the prestigious Carnegie Hall, one of his most victorious moments, no more a struggling pianist in the shadows of New York City - now a legend!

Van Cliburn Performing in the White House East Room

Chapter 22

In Demand

At the age of twenty-three, Van's touring schedule was so tight his manager engaged a private plane to fly Van from concert to concert. His incredibly busy schedule continued for the next twenty years performing at every major venue in the world. The audience could not get enough of Van Cliburn!

As fate moved in an unanticipated direction, Van felt the need to put his career on hold after his father died, but it would not stop him. A repeat experience of performing would eventually occur. Van Cliburn was once again in demand after returning to the stage from taking a hiatus of nine years. He was constantly being asked to play for galas, openings, concerts, or private venues. Many well-known conductors specifically sought out Van and preferred him to play at their symphony concerts. Throughout his life, Van opened many music halls, for he was the drawing attraction. He was a guest soloist in 1968 for the New Garden State Arts Center in New Jersey and in May of 1998 for the Bass Performance Hall in Texas, to name a few.

Van played several times at the White House as well. Unfortunately, he also turned down many concerts, including an invitation to play at the White House shortly after John Kennedy assumed the presidency when Jackie Kennedy herself called and asked him to perform there. Van eventually performed at the Congressional Club for President Kennedy on May 2, 1963.

It wasn't about where to perform. It was about when he should perform. Van always wanted the conditions to be right so the audience would be pleased with his performance. Satisfying his audience was a must!

On one occasion during the winter at the White House, Van agreed to play the American anthem along with other notable classical musicians. The performance was to take place outside in freezing cold temperatures. Besides Van's hands being exposed to the cold weather, the piano on which he was to play was having problems. Eventually, it was decided he would not play, and Van was quite relieved as the conditions were so undesirable for not only a pianist of his caliber, but for his audience.

We were constantly going over the possible dates for upcoming concerts. However, some of these events had to be booked a year or more into the future. Finding an optimal day was crucial to the outcome of each concert played. Sometimes, I worked feverishly with Van. His sense of humor and fascinating stories kept me persevering. I often wondered how lucky I was to be hearing all of Van's stories and how everyone would appreciate them.

Chapter 23

The Early Days

V an knew that he was blessed, yet his parents did such a great job in raising him that it never went to his head. A down-to-earth, charming Texan who was always an engaging inspiration is a description that fits his lively yet cultured personality.

Because of who Van was, he was always in the spotlight. His tall, handsome physique was sure to capture the media's attention. And although he lived a lavish lifestyle, there were several occasions where he did not want to participate in certain events. He so enjoyed the peace and tranquility of his estate in Fort Worth, Texas.

There Van Cliburn lived a humble yet glamorous life, exercising good moral values, kindness, and compassion. Although he worked hard, he knew he was fortunate, and appreciated every day.

Class emanated from Van. It was a rare day indeed if Van lost his composure, for he seemed so collected all of the time. I often felt that he exemplified class not only for himself, but also for what it could do for classical music - his first love. He desired to teach everyone about classical music and how its magnificence would enhance one's life and possibly

54

send the soul into sheer bliss. I was grateful that Van furthered my own education in classical music. There was so much to learn.

Van mentioned many times that when he was asked to give money to different medical or health-related research organizations, his response was that he felt compelled to give to the awareness and appreciation of classical music. For he truly believed that "Without music, there would be nothing to move the spirit, nothing to live for, no hope." The soul must be inspired to live.

Chapter 24

The World as We Know It

S ince Van was well-traveled, with all of the exposure, he was very aware of the world. He was always shocked to hear of the inhumanity that took place on planet Earth and why this had to be. He was extremely sensitive, which contributed keenly to his being a great concert pianist. There were times he could not relate to this planet or what existed here, the atrocities. Everything seemed so alien to him. At times, Van would express to me how he felt he should not be here on Earth. "I feel I don't belong to this world," he would say. His genius sensitivity was not always well-received in a heartless world.

However, Van Cliburn loved beauty, and he was always impressed with his travels to California and the scenic beauty that existed there. He spoke of how Texas had its charm, and New York was a drawing attraction, but he had never seen a state that offered so many lush, scenic views everywhere as California. He always enjoyed traveling there and sometimes performing in Los Angeles, San Francisco, Santa Barbara, and Modesto.

In 1995, Van Cliburn performed at a concert at the San Francisco Opera House, a fully restored building that was damaged in the 1906 devastating earthquake. Van expressed how its dome shape contributes to its wonderful acoustics, which a pianist will always appreciate. Two members of my family attended and could only say, "It was magical!" Van Cliburn had once again created an atmosphere that was mesmerizing. Van was so pleased with the performance he played an encore and garnered several standing ovations that evening. The acoustics play a strong part in how a performing artist is received as the music reverberates off of the walls and ceiling to be heard. Van said he loved playing in the concert hall in Fort Worth, Texas, for that reason alone. He also marveled at the acoustics when playing in Moscow's Music Hall. Music needs to be heard as it was meant to be.

Chapter 25

Azerbaijan

T wo years after Van Cliburn had seized the Gold Medal, he decided to perform in Baku, Azerbaijan on June 28, 1960, at Baku's Philharmonic Hall. It was an unusual request to perform in such a foreign country. However, Van not only experienced an extraordinary performance, but was also received with warmth and deep affection by the Azerbaijan people. They knew Van Cliburn was a music phenomenon and were thrilled that an artist of his worldly status would even consider playing for them. Once again, Van was profoundly moved.

In the autumn of 1995, when Van had an opportunity to play for the country of Azerbaijan again, he jumped at the chance. As we have all walked down memory lane, imagine if this experience occurred in an obscure foreign country. He mentioned to me how there was something about the environment that made him feel right at home. I was envisioning a monumental landmark or maybe a glistening church, but Van was surprised to see how the miles and miles of oil derricks there were so similar to the ones back in Texas, where he had grown up in Kilgore. First viewing them in 1960, their peculiar-looking shapes seemed to line the streets and welcome him back once again. Van said he had beautiful memories of the warm hospitality there. The performance was another success and clearly appreciated by an enthusiastic audience in Azerbaijan who greatly admired Van Cliburn.

Chapter 26

The Audience

Pleasing his audience was what was most important to Van. He would work late into the night and the following morning, practicing for months to prepare for a concert. Many, many times, he would ask if I thought he would have a good practice session, which he would usually do following our midnight sessions. Practicing until 3 am or 4 am in the morning was common. Van and I were both night owls, so I could easily understand his desire to practice so late into the wee hours of the morning so he could dive into his craft without interruption.

Van was also very concerned about the reviews, so we would discuss what the critics might write according to the astrological timing after a concert he had played. Usually, a critic would write his or her review following a concert or in the early morning. I would explain to him astrologically what was occurring at these times so he would know what to expect. Of course, we aimed for the best times and days so that there were not any unexpected surprises.

Van knew a lot of critics by this time, and he blended what I would describe with what he knew of them and their writing criticisms or praise. At times, they were very critical about him expanding his repertoire or classical music experience. Regardless of the comments, Van Cliburn could feel the audience when he played, and in almost every case, he felt he had pleased them. I was pleased to hear that too!

Chapter 27

The Lawsuit

For several years, Van's career was moving along brilliantly after he returned to the stage. I was in the wings, guiding him and thoroughly enjoying our time together. We were able to converse so easily when in each other's company via the phone. Although I worked very hard, the communication between us seemed effortless like we had known each other for lifetimes. Regardless of what kind of relationship you have, communication is everything. This unique rapport was to be treasured for sure, and we both knew it. At the time, I realized that our bond was special, but I would appreciate it even more in the future when Van's presence was languishing.

One evening in mid-July of 1997, Van called to discuss what would be a very draining lawsuit. Van, being a private person, was shocked and humiliated. The situation involved a man hired to manage his and his mother's financial transactions, whom Van had become personally acquainted with and then became unimpressed by his work and protocol. Feeling destabilized, Van ended up firing him for not following through on managing his and his mother's financial affairs. We called him the "kukoo" to devalue his status, but he was much more sinister than the name implies.

Van went through a living hell. I can still hear his deep sighs over the phone. Taking advantage of Van Cliburn was clearly his ultimate and disgusting plan. All he was interested in was Van's money. We worked feverishly for many days and nights and went over several dates to try to unravel where this situation was going and how to best handle it. I finally concluded one night when Van directly asked me to use my intuition and tell him what I thought, that it would be resolved out of court for a specific low settlement amount. Within the next month, Van's attorney negotiated a settlement of the exact amount. Although the case was thrown out of court, Van wanted to protect his future. After this occurrence, Van started relying on my intuitive qualities as well as my astrological advice. I was thankful that I could help him through such a trying time. Although this was a devastating blow, at least he could put it behind him.

There were still many concerts to play, and I encouraged Van to move forward to do what he was born to do - perform classical music!

Several years later, the threatening "kukoo" returned. Van was so under-minded by "him" that he feared some kind of physical retaliation. During this time, we discussed getting a security patrol to look after his home when he was away, which was quite often. Gradually, the fear elapsed until some very adverse astrological aspects came around, and Van would ask me if the "kukoo" would reappear under such nasty astrological influences. I didn't hesitate to let him know if I thought danger was on the horizon.

One day during this worrisome period at a concert, Van's assistant spotted the "kukoo" in the audience. Van was not informed until after the concert for fear it would be too disruptive for him to perform at his best. A security person was engaged to sit behind "him" during the performance.

Luckily, nothing occurred, and "he" never crossed Van's path again. We would continue to look for times when possible harm could strike and prepare accordingly with more security if needed.

When you are a celebrity, you risk the chance of being taken advantage of by those unscrupulous characters around you who are hiding behind their masks. The media, in particular, looking for publicity, will exaggerate an event just to turn heads, never thinking about the damage they are doing to a human being who has given so much to society and the world. Shame to those who expedite such tactics.

Chapter 28

An Unexpected Event

A s Van's focus returned to playing concerts, one night he called and we discussed a local concert series that held some challenges. Van needed to make an appearance at the new Bass Performance Hall on May 8th, 9th, and 10th and perform a full solo recital on Tuesday, May 12th, and another concert with orchestra on Thursday, May 14th in 1998. These were dates he felt obligated to pursue since it was in his home town of Fort Worth, Texas. I could only offer him a perspective on how it may play out and some encouragement.

We both had concerns about May 14th, and this was not a day I would have chosen for him. Although it was rare, occasionally, I was frustrated when Van went forward playing a date that did not agree with him. This date turned out to be one of those ominous days.

Although the earlier recital was performed well, while playing this particular concert, Rachmaninoff Piano Concerto No. 2, the unthinkable happened! Toward the end of the performance, after playing for one and a half hours in front of a packed house, Van Cliburn started to collapse on stage and fainted! I was devastated.

Apparently, unbeknownst to me, there had been a lot of burning in the area, and Van enjoyed taking long walks around the secure neighborhood. Many felt that he had succumbed to smoke inhalation, which would have affected his performance. Most people don't realize how physical it is when you play a concert. Your entire body is involved with playing the music. Van used to spend months preparing for a concert to get his body in shape to perform a piece of music.

Van would not accept payment, a significant amount, even though he played almost the entire composition of music that evening before he started to collapse. This occurrence was also an indication that he was getting older and needed to be more careful in exhausting himself. The conductor of the orchestra had noticed before the performance that Van seemed to lack sufficient rest and thought he was just experiencing a brief memory lapse until he suddenly fell over.

I decided I had to be more direct and not let Van put himself in a situation that was not benefiting him, even if he thought it might be. My strategy changed in how I would guide him through the rest of his days on Earth.

Chapter 29

Moving Forward

A fter Van's health had improved and the legal case was settled, he continued to address getting his financial affairs in order. We discussed various options that he could pursue. Although he was well-off, performing artists still are not paid what they really deserve. Van would jokingly say, "I may have to panhandle along the street!" Often, we would discuss Van's financial situation with stocks, investments, and property to see if there was a way to alleviate some of his concerns.

Van let go of some Boeing stocks, concluded a financial negotiation with South Korea, and in early July, played a concert in San Francisco and, later that month, played a concert in Honolulu. In September, he played in Budapest and then off to Singapore. For some years, while he was continuing to play concerts, we were also thoroughly discussing his finances until he seemed to be getting a better handle on them by 1999.

After a few years of advising Van, I was beginning to understand just how worldly he really was. In doing business with, traveling to, or playing a concert, every place on the planet was an option. I also realized how important my advice was in guiding him. Although I had hundreds of clients, Van started to gradually garner a position at the forefront of my life. He began calling me more and more. Often calling in the afternoon to see if I would be free sometime that evening. There was never a set time, which added to the spontaneity of our sessions.

Van and I became intrigued with each other, which created a tone of excitement whenever we interacted. We so looked forward to speaking to one another. As the years passed, we grew closer and shared so much more. He intuitively made suggestions to me about my own life, such as where to live when I one day might leave New York City. Since I knew he had my best interests at heart, I listened carefully. We supported each other financially, spiritually, and emotionally. It seemed like our affinity with one another would just go on forever.

However, to continue to be effective, I had to keep some distance in order to be objective. The geographical barrier helped, but our bond continued to grow. We could not stop our exceptional rapport and growing fondness for one another.

Chapter 30

One's Personal Life

Van Cliburn was so immersed in the world of classical music that he never wanted anything concerning his personal life to overshadow his love for classical music. He was a very private person, only wanting classical music to be in the limelight. Sexuality has its place in the world, but for Van and I, it was about the music, always about the music. You cannot revere classical music and then let personal issues get in the way. Van believed, that sexuality is not what you represent as a person. It is your behavior and, therefore, does not merit a position in the spotlight.

Although Van and I very rarely talked about sex, we respected one's choices. Whoever you were with, as long as children were not involved, was your business. As the years passed, we gradually shared more and more with each other. On several occasions, he expressed to me how, in an intimate relationship, "You can't counterfeit love, for love is truth."

Chapter 31

The Conductor, Being Who You Are

After ten years of encouraging and guiding Van Cliburn's life, he started speaking to me about moving to Russia. He loved it so, and wanted to live out his final days there. At that time, there were certain astrological influences in Van's chart that indicated it should be considered. We discussed where he would live and what he would do there. Van felt it was an opportunity for him to conduct.

Contrary to what some will have you believe, Van's major ambition, besides being a phenomenal classical pianist, was to conduct. He studied conducting with Bruno Walter, from 1958 to 1962. Mr. Walter conducted the Los Angeles Philharmonic in December of 1962 with Van Cliburn as soloist in Brahm's Piano Concerto No. 2. Van learned more than a great deal from Mr. Walter.

When scheduled to play at a memorial concert after conductor, Dmitri Mitropoulos had passed away, the inconceivable occurred! Van was to perform Liszt with conductor, Leopold Stokowski at Carnegie Hall when Mr. Stokowski had an unfortunate accident and had to cancel. This was Van Cliburn's chance to prove himself as a real conductor. On very short notice, Van was asked to play and conduct the Concerto No. 3 by Prokofiev! Maestro Mitropoulos had played and conducted this exceptional piece of music many times.

Van dived into this huge undertaking and thoroughly enjoyed himself! The evening concert was such a wonderful success that Mr. Cliburn received many invitations to conduct concerts, which he was terribly eager to do. In fact, from 1961 to 1966, Van Cliburn conducted 27 times with some very prestigious orchestras: New York Philharmonic, Philadelphia Orchestra, Dallas Symphony, Leningrad Philharmonic, and the Moscow Philharmonic to name a few.

With his past experience and love of conducting, Van felt that if he moved, he would conduct in Russia or wherever he was led in the world. Whether conducting or playing the piano, there is no doubt Van Cliburn would have been well-received, especially by the country that cherished him – Russia!

Chapter 32

Van Loved Russia

Although Van Cliburn was a sworn Texan, he loved Russia. He looked forward to every visit. Unlike Americans, they appreciated his every note when played on the piano. The one point that Russians have over the Americans is their thorough appreciation of the arts. Van Cliburn was the exception.

The stage would be covered with flowers before he even started to play. He was humbled when showered with gifts of all kinds. People's jewelry and keepsakes were often given to him. He treasured them all. "Russia was a joy for me! I always loved playing there."

Van adored Russia. It was his home away from home. He loved the Russian people. With their sensitive and highly artistic awareness, they discovered him. Van Cliburn was theirs! As much as Van was a true Texan, his fondness for Russia never ceased. He truly looked forward to every visit.

Moscow and Saint Petersburg are the cities Van would speak highly of when visiting Russia, often saying how magical they were. Besides embracing the people, Van would always be looking for some memento or antique that he could remember his trip by, and he had an incredible collection of art, mementos, and antiques back in Fort Worth. On one trip in particular, he was attracted to this beautiful candelabra, but wasn't sure whether it was a good time for an investment. After a brief phone call to me, we decided he should purchase the antique, and Van was thrilled.

One afternoon, during a rehearsal for a concert in the main performing hall, Van was very shocked to see that the curtains were drawn away from a large painting of no other than Stalin, himself, the founder of the Soviet Union. Many statues and paintings of Stalin were purposely destroyed in the revolution in 1989, for they were symbols of oppression. Van had played there several times, but the curtains were usually closed, and he never knew what painting existed on the wall. He figured it was the old elite who wanted to keep history restored. Communism was nothing that Van Cliburn embraced since he was a true believer in God. Still, it did not alter his feelings for the Russian people.

Chapter 33

Olga Rostropovich

Socially, during his trips to Russia, Van would enjoy the company of socialite and music director Olga Rostropovich. He had much fun with her, especially on an evening out for dinner one night. He mentioned how Olga is "revered in Russia like royalty," being the daughter of the famous Russian cellist and conductor Mstislav Rostropovich. "When we walked into a restaurant with Olga on my arm, everyone clapped, and I said to myself, now that's very impressive." What a sense of humor, I thought.

Olga would continue to support Van and his career. One spring day, Olga called and wanted Van to teach a master class and also perform in Russia. Van was very interested in teaching the master class as he wanted all students to have an appreciation for classical music. However, he did not want to perform. Instead, Van was able to arrange for a talented, young pianist to perform a concert for everyone.

During this time, the astrology was very challenging as a phenomenon called Mercury retrograde was occurring. Van was concerned that he would be overlooked or not highly appreciated by the Russian people. We decided he should go since there was an encouraging astrological transit for teaching the youth, which is what he would be doing. Once the decision was made, we planned out everything. When Van arrived in Russia, he had to seriously maintain his concentration and keep up with the teaching schedule. The more pressing task was keeping a low profile, which was very unlike his character. Fortunately, all went well and Van looked forward to his next traveling experience.

Chapter 34

Trip to Russia

In a warm June of 2004, Van Cliburn called to discuss a trip to Moscow to receive The Order of Friendship Award, for which he was deeply grateful. We discussed every day of his trip quite thoroughly, from taking off to landing to checking in, to the best concert playing days, to publicity, to receiving the award, to traveling inside the country, and lastly, to flying home. Every detail, as usual, was covered. When Van arrived at his hotel, he said his room was filled with flowers galore. Gratifying one's spirit, he always felt welcomed in Russia.

Van received the Order of Friendship award on September 20th at 1:45 pm Moscow time in the Kremlin. The following evening, on September 21st, at 7:30 pm, he played a concert that he said "went beautifully!"

Van felt he had an amicable rapport with Vladimir Putin and appreciated the rare interactions that they had when he was playing a concert in Russia. He was fulfilled with this trip, saying, "The Russian soul loves classical music! They receive classical music like no other country."

Van called me on 9/26 at 5:15 pm and 9/27 at 9:39 am. He exclaimed, "This has been the most magical trip! Everything has been so pleasant and fulfilling, but I don't know when I have expended so much physical and psychic energy on a trip." He also said he had played at the Pushkin Museum and found himself to be very exhausted.

Van continued saying, "They are thinking of starting a school here. I may be getting a place in Russia. Gorbachev offered me a small house for me to buy, but I turned him down. This trip has been very fateful, just like you said it would be." He continued saying, "My soul is Russian."

Whether Van should move to Russia or not was part of our discussion for several years. He had so many responsibilities it was difficult to plan a huge move of this kind. Thus, it never occurred.

I was extremely pleased with the outcome of Van's honorary trip to Russia. After all, that was my job.

Chapter 35

Presidents

W hen you are dealing with the presidency of the United States, which Van Cliburn, having played for seven presidents, was accustomed to, security is the rule. An intense protocol was always in effect around the White House.

On May 2nd, 1963, Van Cliburn met and played for John F. Kennedy at a Congressional Club Breakfast at the John F. Kennedy Library. Almost seven months later, on November 22nd 1963, at half past noon, President Kennedy was assassinated in Dallas, Texas. Van Cliburn was totally shocked, like most Americans. Almost cancelling, he decided to continue with his plans to attend the San Francisco Opera with Mary Costa performing that evening. He sat with Samuel Barber, a noted composer in his own right, whose works Van appreciated playing throughout his illustrious career. Later, he retired at the Beverly Hills Hotel, a place that he enjoyed staying at whenever possible, giving great thought to the direction of our country.

In February of 1964, shortly after President Johnson assumed his position, Van was asked to come and perform at the White House. Washington, D.C., was still under strict martial law. They were not taking any chances. Van commented. "There were tanks surrounding the capital that were 25 feet apart. I have never seen so much security! I even had to drive in a specially designated white house car." Van went on to respectfully play a recital. He was usually comfortable in visiting the white house, which he had done many times playing for several presidents, from Truman to Obama, but never under such incredibly intense conditions.

Chapter 36

An Evening at the White House

R egardless of where Van Cliburn was performing, he continued to have a special relationship with Russia, the country that discovered him. After the era of communism in Russia, the anthem was changed. Van commented one evening saying, "In 1991, Russia went back to using the old anthem, and the people went crazy." "Except for some of the rich folk, it reminded them of communism, but I think it is beautiful." Moscow Nights, another song that was written and composed in 1955, was a piece of music that Van Cliburn appreciated so much he played it at the Tchaikovsky Competition, where he won the gold medal.

When Van returned to the stage in 1987 after a nine-year absence, he was invited by Nancy and Ronald Reagan to play at the White House. Van was to perform for Mikhail Gorbachev and his wife and the Reagan's for a formal, intimate gathering one evening.

After playing his assigned pieces, Van went on to improvise, playing as well as singing "Moscow Nights," a true favorite in Russia. The Reagan's were totally surprised, and Gorbachev and his wife were completely delighted and started singing the song right along with him! Gorbachev was thrilled, and Van's warm gesture clearly moved the discussion of politics in a positive direction. Who would have had the courage to go impromptu and play the Cold War Russian "Moscow Nights?" No one, but Van Cliburn! It was another step toward ending the "Cold War" through the beauty of classical music and the genius of Van Cliburn.

Chapter 37

Gatherings at the Ranch

P erforming at the white house for another president and his wife, Laura and President George Bush was definitely a highlight for Van Cliburn. He thoroughly appreciated their company and often commented on what wonderful people they were. Since they all lived in Texas, there was a natural camaraderie. He played in the East Room at the white house several times, besides attending other formal occasions.

One evening, Van called me to discuss an invitation by President George Bush to a barbecue at the Crawford Ranch in Texas, which President Vladimir Putin would be attending as well. Van was pleasantly surprised when he was asked to join the afternoon event on November 14, 2001. We discussed what would transpire so Van was prepared for the influential gathering.

President Putin would always respectfully acknowledge Van when he performed in Russia, at times even in person. So, Van was very comfortable in his company. As Van Cliburn, through classical music, helped end the "cold war", President Bush knew that having Van Cliburn there could influence the Russian President toward hammering out a nuclear missile deal, which was the real reason for winning and dining President Putin at the vast ranch. At this time, it was crucial that nuclear disarmament was pursued, thus cutting back on nuclear defense for both highly militarily armed countries.

Although there might be some unwanted tension between the two leaders, to Van Cliburn, President Putin was very approachable. Van, in his natural manner, had a way with people in being so genuinely warm and friendly that he would "break the ice" every time. At such a gathering, breaking down any barriers, just as he had accomplished in winning the gold medal in Russia, was more than appreciated. Van's lively persona was witty, humorous, classy, and honest, and a delight to have around when intense politics permeated the air. Hence, his presence was a very desired commodity. Even though the stakes were high, Van Cliburn thoroughly enjoyed himself by just being himself and changed the dynamics to a much more receptive political agenda. Nuclear disarmament would ensue.

Chapter 38

Speaking In Code

S ince Van was in the white house performing for most of the presidents that lived during his career, you would expect some surveillance. Our phone lines were always being tapped. It was very obvious when the government was listening in, and I could think of several times when Van suggested we get off the phone since he felt he was sharing too much information with me, and he would call me later that evening. "Christine, do you hear that?" Van would say. "Let me call you later."

We also started speaking in code. There were keywords for many individuals he would associate with, especially those in the White House. Sometimes, he would unexpectedly bring up a coded name, and I had to figure it out by the context of our conversation. Since I was using my brain capacity to its fullest in guiding Van, I could certainly address decoding his thoughts.

Having your lines tapped at times was annoying, but you learn to live with it. Neither of us had any fear, nor were we going to completely stop our discussions because of an announced listening ear. The importance of our meetings far outweighed a government intruder.

Chapter 39

The Meeting

I will never forget our first meeting in person. On the phone one evening, Van exclaimed, "I want to meet you!" Since he was coming to New York City soon, where I lived on the Upper West Side, we arranged a date. We met at the elegant Hotel Pierre right off Central Park. I was led into the room where he was enjoying a cigarette. Van loved to smoke. Somehow, it seemed to calm him and allow him to think at his best. Van also used an aqua filter for many years to help curb the ravishing effects that smoking could bring. "Since 1964, I never smoked a cigarette without an aqua filter."

Van rose and gave me the warmest hug and then meticulously watched me with such intensity and curiosity in his eyes as if he was trying to figure me out. I could almost hear his mind say, who is this woman that he connected so extremely well with and told his secrets to without hesitation? We were intrigued with each other over the phone, and now we were intrigued with each other in person. We had an exceptionally pleasant evening, discussing whatever came to mind, and then Van took me home in his limousine. He carefully watched my entrance into the building where I lived at 200 West 60th Street, as if he was trying to get one more glimpse of who I was.

I was glad to have met Van Cliburn in person, but I also knew that my role in his life was behind the scenes. I did not have to be in Van's presence, for I felt his presence all of the time.

Shortly thereafter, on another visit to New York City, Van called and invited me to a memorial for a special friend at the Metropolitan Museum in New York City. Van played a special piece of music, and I met him afterwards. So humble was he that he apologized for not being on his game with his performance. I looked back at him and said while he was giving me a hug, "You were absolutely great!" He then went out into the audience, where he was showered with affection. Van was so magnetic that people were stunned by his overwhelming presence, which filled the entire room.

I only saw Van play in person this one time, for I often felt that if I interacted with Van too much, I would not be able to be objective with him in our sessions. I'm sure he felt the same way, for we could have met up in New York City on several occasions and did not, but I always heard from him. There were three things I could rely on while living in New York City for thirty years: feeling optimistic, prospering in my work, and Van Cliburn calling.

Chapter 40

Around the World

I f Van was not playing a concert somewhere in the world, he was likely traveling to a specific destination to improve his interaction with everyone, including his audience. Every month, a new astrology chart comes into play and is set into motion on a particular day, time, and place. Thus, I was advising Van to fly to many places around the globe for the best results. We had a great time plotting what city he would fly to next for his monthly astrology chart. I always looked for the most auspicious places. We were both thrilled with the fact that in selecting a specific location, the world was our oyster. As an astrologer, who could ask for more?!

I was very precise in my calculations, and in charting the best locations, there were times Van would end up in places that were out of the norm, such as Hapeville, PA or Plano, TX or Castle Park, CA. or Pensacola, FL. His preferred places of travel included Prague, Puerto Vallarta, Cabo San Lucas, and New York. His concerts were in cities everywhere: San Francisco, Los Angeles, Modesto, Salt Lake City, Chicago, New York City, Tanglewood, Boston, Washington, DC, Fort Worth, Dallas, Tokyo, Moscow,

Saint Petersburg, Olga, Prague, London, Paris, Frankfurt, Athens, and many more.

Van Cliburn played five times at the Pantheon in Athens, Greece. He commented on how it really takes you back to the time BC. One night, he surreptitiously went back to the Pantheon after he had played a concert there to experience the historical ambience of the ancient arena. Van surprisingly encountered the secret police looking after the place. He had to quickly explain who he was so they did not look upon him with suspicion and end up behind bars!

After having a triumphant win in Moscow in 1958, Van Cliburn had a rigorous touring schedule for 20 years that included destined performing venues around the world. Now, his future schedule was different as every event became an extensively planned itinerary that seriously involved my guidance.

Following his nine-year hiatus, Van's schedule was also not quite as demanding so he became very selective about the dates he would play. Still, Van was especially busy in 2002 – 2003, where he played concerts in Vancouver, CAN – April 25, 2002, Washington DC – June 10, 2002, Richardson, TX – September 19, 2002, Hattiesburg, MI – November 7, 2002, Seattle. WA – February 27, 2003. Salt Lake City, UT – March 18, 2003, and Birmingham, AL – April 10, 2003.

Whenever Van could, he would play on his desired piano. Shipping his instrument, a Steinway grand piano, to all of these places was quite a feat! Traveling overseas, he did not always have that luxury, but he would request a Steinway piano to be tuned and ready to play upon his arrival.

One evening, he called to discuss a series of four concerts to be played in Japan starting December 3, 2006. Since Van Cliburn's Legendary Visions DVD has optional Japanese subtitles, he was thrilled to perform there. Van commented on how gracious the Japanese people were and how he thoroughly enjoyed meeting the royal couple. "They treated me with great respect," he said. The concerts went well and Van was invigorated by the whole experience. He was also pleased to see how much the Japanese culture truly appreciated classical music, a reflection of their deep spiritual essence as shown in their masterful artwork and Kabuki theatre.

Chapter 41

The Social Scene

V an Cliburn had quite an elaborate social life, but no one knew him quite the way I did. He let his guard down with me and went on and on about what was on his mind. I made every effort to address his concerns. Some people would like to say in his decision-making, Van just wanted confirmation from me. Sometimes, that was the case, but more often than not I carefully advised him.

Van would also share much with his good friend Patsy Pope. He was more than happy to be her escort at the 87th Opera House Gala in San Francisco. A wonderful gift of 40 million dollars was donated by John A. and Cynthia Gunn to the San Francisco Opera. Besides humanity, there's nothing better than to give to the arts, which Van Cliburn was totally devoted to doing.

Many celebrities, leaders, and presidents crossed Van's path, but only a few will I mention. There were two friends that he spoke highly of, Angie Dickinson and Linda Evans. He always appreciated when they had an opportunity to get together, usually at a social engagement or dinner party.

One day, he encouraged me to watch a particular movie that Ms. Dickinson was in, commenting on what a great acting job she did. I remember her as a policewoman, breaking down the barriers for women everywhere. Angie Dickinson would also have dinner with Van Cliburn for the last time, twelve days before Van passed away. I am sure she is grateful she made the effort to see her good friend for the last time. Van was very pleased she found the time to share special memories with him.

Leontyne Price and Van were friends for years. Van mentioned that they made their debut on the same day. At one of her performances, Van exclaimed, "She hit high C at the end of the acapella song, and it was breathtaking!" "I sent her flowers." Years later, on January 24, 2008, Van gave a special speech at the Pierre Hotel in New York City honoring Leontyne Price and her remarkable, legendary career. Once again, Van was enthralled with a prominent, classical female singer, his inspiration.

Van was invited to the white house to play several times in his career. On one occasion, when he attended a white house dinner, he was pleasantly surprised by the entertainment of a quartet with Condoleezza Rice, secretary of state at the time, at the piano. Van was impressed and said, "She did quite well." He appreciated Condoleezza Rice for the woman that she was, a woman of distinction.

Chapter 42

Shaking Hands

V an expressed to me one evening that in Texas, where Van resided, your word and a handshake were as good as a contract. There was a certain understanding that one did not renege on in this traditional custom used more often as a greeting.

As Van was very social, a polite, social decorum comes with the gesture of shaking hands. Although appreciative of the gesture, Van would try to avoid shaking hands as he had to keep his delicate playing hands from being compromised by an overly aggressive handshake. He mentioned how some people, especially men, had such a strong grip when shaking hands that he was concerned it would end up affecting his playing. When he could easily greet 10, 20, 30 or more people at a time, I could see why he would be concerned.

Van preferred a European hug, where he would place his hands on someone's upper arms and lean into them slightly. Upon meeting up with Van after a performance one afternoon at the Metropolitan Museum in New York City, he was pleased to see me as he had extended an invitation to come to his performance. He proceeded to give me a warm hug, which I was expecting. As I moved over to allow those in the audience to greet him, Van continued with one hug after another. As a Cancerian in the zodiac signs, hugging others was very apropos for Van. However, I chuckled to myself, knowing what was really behind the warm gesture.

Chapter 43

His English Home

Much socializing would occur at Van's desired residence as well. Van expressed to me that in 1985, after seeing a beautiful, English-looking home in Fort Worth, Texas, he decided to go ahead with the purchase. Rildia Bee Cliburn, Van's mother, also loved the home and thought it would be the perfect place for Van. As it turned out, it was.

The real estate deal went through on October 31st, 1985. Van and I studied the astrology chart several times to see if there was any indication of him one day selling the place and leaving Fort Worth. Van had a strong desire to move to Russia, but he never did. In fact, during the last four years of his life, he said many times, "I don't see myself leaving this home."

The house was a desired property, especially because of its spectacular view. Gardens, a gazebo, and eventually, a library would adorn the estate. Inside, memorabilia, photos specifically placed, chandeliers, and incredible works of art were everywhere. And, of course, almost every room had a grand piano. In fact, this three-story, Tudor-style mansion proudly displayed nine grand pianos at one time!

Van loved to entertain, and the exquisite property was perfect for the many, many dinner parties over the years. We would look for the most optimal days and nights to have his guests over. Sometimes, the dates were chosen for him as someone was in town for a brief stay. We would carefully go over the daily transits to see if there were any supportive influences or surprises and to avoid times that were not so favorable.

I always advised Van to avoid negative periods throughout the day. I would counsel him on the best times to practice, perform, be interviewed, be filmed, travel, make phone calls, and sign contracts so that all would go well. It was intense and exciting all at the same time. In my exhaustion, I also felt great fulfillment in getting the results I wanted for Van. Some days, Van pushed me to my limit to perfect my skills, and we both gained. Our collaboration was a lucky one indeed.

Christine Rakela

Cliburn's Former Tudor Estate

Cliburn's Tudor Garden

Chapter 44

Tanglewood

J uly 23rd, 1966, in Tanglewood was a day to remember, especially if you were sitting in the audience listening to Van Cliburn perform Rachmaninoff's Piano Concerto No. 3 in D Minor. Van Cliburn's performance was flawless! It was a repeat performance of his victory win in Moscow eight years earlier. Over fourteen thousand people were ecstatic!

Van Cliburn told me how he thoroughly enjoyed performing at Tanglewood, as there was something special about it. Perhaps being one with nature under the stars created an ambiance that allowed the soul to embrace the grandeur of classical music. Van played there several times over his long, illustrious career.

At the beginning of 1998, Van Cliburn called to discuss playing at Tanglewood once again. The date was July 17, 1998. Van was playing fewer concerts at this time and felt the need to take on this date. He was to perform with the Boston Symphony as he had done earlier in his career. The piece was Rachmaninoff's Concerto No. 2.

There were times when Van and I had to work with the dates that were given to him as opposed to manipulating the schedule for the most optimal time. I knew from the start that the astrology would be challenging and clearly indicated he would feel frazzled, especially at the onset of the performance. Gradually, he would find his rhythm.

Although Van always felt stressed before a performance, he would relax into his craft the instant he began to play. That was not the case this particular evening. The audience, however, didn't mind. After all, they were listening to Van Cliburn!

The critics, on the other hand, were not so forgiving. Van was already prepared for their review, as we could tell by the astrological influences the next day that they were going to be judgmental. Van was also aware of certain critics who held back on giving any praise, even if it was due. Although Van still did a fabulous job, the compliment was not forthcoming. One has to keep in mind that critics are just that, critics. Van told me that he played what the people wanted to hear, not what the critics wanted.

Chapter 45

Timing the Honorary Doctorate Degree

There would be many accolades for Van Cliburn's achievements. Van received an honorary doctorate degree from the Cleveland Institute of Music at their 87th annual commencement, which he was very pleased to acknowledge. He then addressed the graduates in his pure Van Cliburn style with his inspiring words in a speech that was always exceptional. However, to get to the event on time, we had to schedule everything like clockwork.

Getting Van to the state of Ohio to receive his Honorary Doctorate Degree was quite a strategic move. We had to work with the timing on his monthly astrology chart, called the lunar return, by sending him from Fort Worth to a small airport outside of Georgia called Hapeville, where he stayed the night. Here, Van would experience his lunar return early in the morning. Then, from there, get him back on a private plane to Cleveland, Ohio, to receive his honorary degree in the afternoon, and then back on the plane that same day to Washington, DC, for an engagement at the White House in the evening.

All of this had to take place in a 24-hour period. And, yes, we did it! Van was very pleased with how we pulled it off. He was also very grateful for the Honorary Doctorate Degree, acknowledging his expertise as a world-renowned classical pianist. Through the years, Van Cliburn received over twenty doctorate degrees. Such impressive recognition speaks for itself.

Chapter 46

Tithing

A lthough Van Cliburn was in a position of great stature, his generosity was overwhelming at times. Besides giving financially to the arts, Van believed in tithing as well. He faithfully tithed 10% of his income every year. Sometimes Van would comment on how some well-to-do politicians were not so generous, but literally hoarded their money. Other politicians he was impressed with as their contributions to society were quite generous. He clearly felt that tithing made for a fuller life because you gave back to the world.

When CBS bought Steinway, the piano company, they called Van and asked why Steinway was apparently buying up pianos at around $1800 each. Hearing this news, Van decided to act on this opportunity. At the time, there were two acquaintances that Van knew who wanted pianos. Van decidedly purchased two pianos and gave the pianos to them anonymously. He never told them. Somehow, he managed to keep this to himself without them ever realizing the pianos came from him. Van felt he had served a good purpose. Giving has its own wonderful rewards

Chapter 47

The Van Cliburn Foundation Lives on

E stablishing the Van Cliburn Foundation and the Van Cliburn Piano Competition would not only contribute to his legacy, but perhaps more importantly give eager artists a chance to display their skills and talents, besides bringing a spotlight to the appreciation and importance of classical music in one's life.

The Van Cliburn International Piano Competition was first held in 1962. At the time, Van was twenty-seven years old. In astrology, when one reaches their 27th - 29th birthday, there is a planetary effect called one's Saturn return, where the individual is encouraged to create a stronger foundation in life by taking on more responsibility. The astrology was a direct correlation to starting the Van Cliburn Foundation and Piano Competition.

Van was totally dedicated to the Foundation, and he would do anything to keep it prospering. Saying, "I would rather be eating off of paper plates and plastic forks and knives to have more money for the Foundation."

There were times, however, when the overwhelming responsibilities of the Foundation took their toll on Van. Yet he continued to be of service, regardless of the intense pressure. He had much to say about the winners. Whether being critical or not, he knew that their future would not be an easy one.

Chapter 48

The Grand Staff

V an served on the National Endowment Fund for six years. "I was very loyal and fulfilled my responsibility." He hoped that one-day classical music would be in all of the schools, saying, "We need mandatory music in schools, especially learning about the grand staff. It should be a requirement. They cannot graduate unless they know and understand the grand staff, for classical music is forever!" He continued saying, "When I went to Russia in 1958, everyone knew classical music. Even Khrushchev knew classical music!" No wonder why Van Cliburn was discovered in Russia. The people were educated in music, classical music, that is. Such was the intense bond between Van Cliburn and Russia.

Although he lived in Fort Worth, Texas, his home town where he wanted to please his audience, in Russia, he felt he must satisfy his audience. Van never wanted to let the Russian people down, and every time he journeyed to his beloved Russia, we spent hours, days, and weeks finding the optimal time astrologically that he could go and do his absolute best. It was quite a project, but I, too, shared in his dream of wanting his performances to be absolutely exceptional and, therefore, put classical music in the spotlight, where it deserved to be.

Chapter 49

The Speech-Giver

Whether performing on the piano or giving speeches, Van wanted to do his best. Besides his genius ability on the piano, Van Cliburn fortunately loved to give speeches. He always wanted to open up people's minds and instill inspiration and good sense. In all of his speeches, Van wrote in a fashion that caused people to stop, think, and be inspired. Quite frankly, Van was the best speechwriter, and I was fortunate enough to hear all of his polished, printed works for almost two decades.

He would always run his personally written speech by me before attending an event. His speeches were well thought-out, meaningful, yet entertaining. He was clever in being able to tell a story or describe an event that would leave one pondering the moment about what had just been said. I was always impressed with how his search for the right words created a mosaic composition and his delivery that would surprise many a listener. Van had such a great presence, but when he spoke, his radiant, rich voice filled the room like the acoustics from his piano.

Van expressed to me how, in a past interview, a female writer stated that he possessed impeccable grammar. He said, "My parents really pushed me to speak correctly." By the way Van spoke, he encouraged me to do the same.

People were especially impressed at how Van could deliver a speech so eloquently and have such an impact. Upon giving a brief speech for a Hollywood crowd, several notable names told him afterward that they not only enjoyed his speech, but took note of his outstanding voice. One well-known film director specifically said, "You should consider being in film!" As Van had wanted to become more involved with doing some roles in movies, he was thrilled. He felt that he would be great at being an old man and describing the story of a great musician, not necessarily himself. He so wanted classical music to be in the spotlight, and what a great format to be in the movies! Although this dream never materialized in Van's time, I'm sure his own incredible life story is worth telling on the screen.

Van Cliburn

Photo Courtesy of The Cliburn

Chapter 50

The Pause

V an Cliburn and I were usually in constant contact over the almost 20 years that we orchestrated his life. However, there was one period that caused a lapse in our connection.

In 2010, exhausted from a long-distance move from New York City to California and raising my medically special needs child, I contracted pneumonia. It was a challenging time, and during this period I did not hear from Van Cliburn. We had had several prior conversations shortly before this upset in my life, and I figured he was just busy. I had very little energy to tackle his intriguing yet demanding phone sessions.

Gradually, my health improved and I decided to reconnect with Van. Being an astrologer, I carefully synchronized the date and time I would call Van Cliburn. Knowing his daily routine also helped. On January 20th at 5:30 pm PST, I picked up the phone and dialed Van's number. I knew without a doubt I would reach him.

Van answered the phone, and before I could even say hello, he exclaimed, 'Christine, how are you?!" Thrilled to hear from me, we arranged for a session that evening. It was as if we had never stopped talking. As usual, we picked up from there like there had been no separation between us.

We briefly discussed why some time had passed. I discovered that Van was experiencing his own difficulties. I never told him how ill I had been as an astrologer never wants you to know their weaknesses. Yet, I remember him saying he always knew when I was sick or away. We were so in sync it was uncanny. At times, he could literally read my thoughts and vice versa. We eagerly sought out the stars as well as each other's enjoyable company late into the night. There wasn't a moment to spare.

Chapter 51

An Astrologer's Role

E ven if you love doing astrology readings, they can become very taxing. The person you are counseling can't help but siphon off your energy so they can sustain themselves through what they are going through. It's part of the job. You have to be resilient so you don't become overly exhausted and therefore no good for anyone, including yourself.

Van, however, was the exception to the rule. He knew that life had blessed him with great honor, prestige, and appreciation of his talent, and he never was condescending to anyone. He hoped, however, that the less fortunate or downtrodden would somehow want to make their life better and strive for more.

Van was incredibly vibrant, and his storytelling had me smiling or totally intrigued as I worked diligently through the night to offer him guidance. Although I used a lot of mental energy, I was also exhilarated by our exchange. Besides inspiring, Van was a wonderful human being that I was so grateful to know.

Van was also very sensitive to sound. This was obvious in watching him play, how his entire body could feel the music. He was extremely insightful and would always comment on what a soothing voice I had and how it would help reassure him. Sometimes, he would call and say, "I just had to hear your voice." I had heard from many people that there was something about my voice that put them at ease and gave them reassurance that somehow, regardless of their circumstances, everything would be alright. I was glad the sound of my voice could bring some peace to Van's busy and sometimes extremely overwhelming life.

Chapter 52

Being the Best You Can Be

V an possessed the ability to bring out the best in people, thus, he was so well-liked. He also encouraged people toward civility, something that is so lacking in our society today, yet is priceless on its own merit. When civil, there is a certain decorum one exercises to enhance the soul through kindness and politeness. This has nothing to do with one's background or upbringing, although these issues can certainly influence one in a particular direction. Exercising civility and showing respect for one another can only lead to a better society. Van commented on how we should strive toward improving ourselves. I shared the same thoughts.

Some men know how to bring out the best in a woman, like Fred Astaire for Ginger Rogers. He truly complimented her. Van always brought out the best in me, and I will always be thankful for his acknowledgement of my skills and talents. Van allowed me to rise to my highest good in just the way he interacted with me. He was blessed in the way that his enlightened manner brought out the best in everyone he encountered.

He spoke highly of those who tried to be the best they could be. In one conversation, he mentioned how a popular television host consistently aimed to improve her life. Van greatly admired her for her personal accomplishments. Bringing out your finest self is the most attractive quality in a human being.

In exercising my finest self, I never shied away from the responsibility of collaborating with Van, I embraced it. Being grateful for my advice, every Christmas Van would send me a lovely poinsettia, always signing it, "Much Love, VAN CLIBURN". It was a sweet gesture of appreciation for my hard work for him. He was a true gentleman, thanks to the chivalry instilled in him by his beloved father.

Chapter 53

The Green Room

Having a cultured approach, Van Cliburn truly adored female singers. However, he would often say, "There are two kinds of singers: those who sing and those who sing and know the instrument."

On one occasion at the New Jersey Arena, he happened to share a "green room" with none other than Judy Garland. She was pleased to meet Van, and he was delighted to meet her.

Judy explained at one point, in their brief conversations as they were preparing for an evening of entertainment, "My big disappointment is that I never learned how to read music." An experienced classical artist like Van could only respond by saying, "Wouldn't you have wanted to learn music?" Van encouraged people everywhere to learn more about the intricacies of music for you would only be able to appreciate it that much more.

As talented as Judy Garland was, Van was surprised at her hesitation to pursue music further, but her musical acting career never evolved in that direction. In her response, she reminded Van that he was lucky to be able to surround himself with music all of the time. It wasn't that she didn't want to, the opportunity of understanding music was just not encouraged in her industry.

Considering that Ms. Garland sang so beautifully without knowing some of the fundamentals of music makes one realize just how incredibly talented she actually was. Regardless of her deferred musical knowledge, Van still greatly admired Ms. Garland, as he did all seriously accomplished female singers.

Chapter 54

Las Vegas Venue

All the hoopla makes Las Vegas a great place to perform, but when presented to Van Cliburn by one of the casino resort owners, he had reservations about playing there. "Is this the right venue?" he kept asking. So many artists, including Liberace, have performed at this hot spot for entertainment. Van continued to feel reluctant about proceeding with scheduling a date to perform.

At the request of a casino resort owner, he decided to fly in and check it out for himself. Passing by a restaurant close to the performance auditorium, what seemed like a brawl was underway. Van felt that this atmosphere would cheapen the enlightenment of classical music. He finally withdrew from the offer. With such a variety of entertainment going on, Van felt that it would be difficult to convince those in attendance of the importance of classical music in their lives. Listening to classical music is not a fly-by-night experience. Its sounds allow one to connect with their soul. Without this connection, how can man and womankind look beyond their existence? Classical music is in a class by itself, and for good reason.

Chapter 55

A Good Friend

When you walk into the Metropolitan Opera House in New York City, you are reminded of the classics. Behind the scenes, its financial obligations were addressed by a wealthy, philanthropic couple, whose generosity paid off the debt at the Metropolitan Opera House for millions of dollars. They were also good friends and neighbors of Van Cliburn.

When many of Van's precious items were being auctioned off at Christie's Auction House in New York City, there was a particular silver culinary item that Van hated to give up, but through some convincing did. His neighbor surprised Van one day with her purchase of the silver culinary item worth several thousands of dollars and said he could come over anytime for dinner and view it. Van was thrilled, and so appreciated the warm gesture. That's what friends are for.

Chapter 56

The Billionaires

In a secluded area of Fort Worth, Van's neighbors were all billionaires. He would often-times comment on how he was the little guy in the neighborhood, saying, "I'm the poor man on the block. Everyone around me is a billionaire!" Fortunately for Van, living next to him were an aristocratic couple that were good friends of Van's. He would socialize with them often when they were in town. Van was always grateful that their estate had excellent security that covered some of his property as well.

Although Van Cliburn was living in the land of billionaires, he was in a league of his own, being far more cultured and spiritual than his friends and associates.

Van used to tell me that nothing matters more than being a cultured person. "Money cannot buy class or cultural awareness. Mother always pointed out to me, see that family, they may have money, but they are not cultured. Others don't have money, but they're cultured."

Living among billionaires, you would think that Van Cliburn would appreciate such, but he was unimpressed with just people's money.

Chapter 57

Steinway and Poetry

A s a cultured artist, the two main industries that Van Cliburn endorsed, at the request of his mother, were Steinway Pianos and RCA, with whom he had a lengthy relationship. Since Van Cliburn endorsed Steinway Pianos, he became acquainted with Mrs. Steinway. One day, she shared her favorite poem with him, God's World by Edna St. Vincent Malay. "Oh world, I cannot hold thee close enough! ..."

Van thoroughly enjoyed poetry and was actually the author of some excellent poems, as well as quotes. One evening Van read to me his poem, "Steal Not Away." Having studied poetry throughout my life, I was delighted. I remember thinking how it flowed so beautifully and was emotionally moving, as Van Cliburn always wanted.

"Steal Not Away"

By Van Cliburn

Steal not away, O pierced heart

From all life's mist of treasures,

Of song and dance and worldly pleasures

To escape this fury in silent depart.

Flee thou not, thou bleeding heart

From all life's tribulation,

But on the morrow, take consolation

In the beauty that thou art.

And the empyreal choirs will sing in the empyreal rooms

And their song will be our song.

Just for us - us two.

But, will it be for us only, till there be no tombs

To cover us, and time will ne'er be long

For us - too?

Cliburn's Steinway Piano

Chapter 58

Politics, The Dilemma

A t first, after his world acclaim, Van wasn't in a position to have a voice in politics as classical music was his message, but he would be in the future.

Because Van's travels took him to many political places, politics entered into the picture. Van was very concerned about the direction of our country, the United States of America. He wished he could educate the youth about what is going on in the world besides teaching them some etiquette, which he felt they truly needed. Van would jokingly say, "I wish I could knock some sense into their heads." In one conversation, he stated, "The masses don't understand the volatility of radical Islam. Over three hundred million people here, and most seem unaware. They need to wake up from the dream." The rise of terrorism must be dealt with efficiently. In early 2000, Van was very concerned about the tactics of terrorism and how it needed to be completely eradicated. Otherwise, we would suffer the consequences. He could not have been more accurate.

Closer to home, there was a very heated and sometimes contentious political campaign. However, when two good friends are running for governor in

Texas, and both want you to endorse them, what are you to do?

This is the dilemma that Van had to confront. After speaking to me in depth about the situation, Van finally decided that he respected both of them so much and honored their friendship that he would not be able to endorse either one of them. I was impressed with his wise approach. Thus, he was able to keep the friendship of both candidates. Sometimes, choosing sides isn't always the right answer. In this particular case, putting friendship before politics was the true gain. Although Van always had an abundance of gratification socially, his performance agenda only became more challenging. The stress he carried continued to slowly consume him.

Chapter 59

The Last Concert Performance

On September 15, 2007, in Buffalo, New York, Van played a concert that was very stressful, after not having played in a while. Still, the concert was a success, but this experience gradually led to Van's retirement.

During this year, Beverly Sills, one of the most famous opera singers, passed away, leaving many precious memories of great performances. I can't help but think that, somehow, this impacted Van and his love for female opera singers.

Sure enough, on October 2nd, 2007, Van Cliburn walked off the stage after playing a concert performance and told his assistant, "This is the last concert I will ever play."

His loyal assistant tried to convince him that that was not the case, but sadly, it was true. Van uttered the fated words that would play out in his life. He never played another major concert. Van had other concerns on his mind.

Van still played some private engagements, but he preferred to give speeches. He thought he might explore the world of conducting, as he had done earlier in his career, until Ridia Bee, his mother, said, "They are only allowing you to conduct because of how you play the piano." Back then, hearing those words was enough for him to stop, but now he could pursue what he seemed to enjoy. Van continued to perform for private venues, but was also mulling over future possibilities that seemed so distant.

Chapter 60

Music and the Party

I n June of 2001, Van was impressed with another performance. Russian-born, American pianist Olga Kern became the prestigious gold medalist at the Van Cliburn Competition, which is held every four years in Fort Worth, Texas. Van was very pleased with her performance and felt she deserved to win. And winning would catapult her career into the limelight. Ms. Kern also had a son.

On a warm summer day in 2011, there was a well-attended party at the Van Cliburn estate, and Olga Kern's son, Vladislav Kern, played on the piano. Van expressed how good he was at performing, a potential prodigy perhaps, who seemed to be following in his mother's footsteps as a world class pianist.

Van's assistant had this incredible library built where the event was being held. Many Fort Worth notables attended. Van raved about the library. I, too, was very impressed when I finally saw it one day.

Van described the gathering as if you were there. "You felt like you were going to heaven - the acoustics were unbelievable! 11,000 red carnations, 4,000 sq. ft, classical music playing throughout the evening."

"The Prime Minister of Russia arrived last night" to attend the event. He presented Van with a calendar, where Van Cliburn is a portrait of every month. Another reminder of just how loved Van Cliburn was in Russia.

Even "Putin sent a beautiful letter." President Vladimir Putin, who was invited to the event, sent the Prime Minister of Russia in his place.

It was a lovely event, filled with an exquisite string quartet and celestial-sounding choir. Although the music that day was inspirational, Van, however, was not in good physical health and barely made it through the event. He was in much pain, especially when walking, but being the actor he was I am sure no one knew. Most of the responsibilities fell on his assistant. Van was thankful he did such a great job and attracted compliments from friends and neighbors.

I had discussed with Van how his health would undergo major challenges during this time period of his life. For the next three years, he would be under difficult planetary conditions. Saturn and Neptune were starting to have adverse effects on the health sector of his astrology chart. These two influences together are very debilitating. Health issues would continue to plague Van. I was extremely concerned and encouraged him to be more aware of his health and get frequent and thorough check-ups from his physician. His astrology led me to believe there was a serious health problem developing. I knew it was going it be a rough period, and together, we would have to navigate Van's life with great caution.

Chapter 61

Writing Down His Thoughts

I t was clear that Van wanted to do so much more with his life. Conducting was always on his mind, but he was also a great writer. Van and I discussed, throughout the years, him writing a book of some kind. He only wanted to write about the intricacies of classical music and how it related to life. In his later years, I encouraged him to pen his thoughts, but he didn't seem to be motivated to pursue this creative goal because of the tremendous stress he was experiencing. Somehow, I always felt there would be time when the stress was alleviated to continue to discuss a writing project, but time eventually ran out.

Van expressed to me one evening, "I want to do something with my life to bring true knowledge to people." As if Van Cliburn had not done enough, he wanted to do more. So many of his thoughts had such an impact on me. I knew the world needed to hear and ponder his true wisdom.

Chapter 62

God and Astrology

Van Cliburn was a church-going man and appreciated the opportunity to conjoin with his creator. At times, he would tell me of special prayer sessions he would have to encourage a better outcome with situations in his life. He also included astrological advice. We both saw God and the proper use of astrology, what God made for mankind, as what would enlarge our experience in life and not to be taken for granted.

In the use of astrology, it wasn't that we didn't believe in God, for we definitely did. For Van and I, God was the ultimate. However, we both knew that God gave us tools to help ourselves on planet Earth, and the mathematics of astrology was one of them.

Van was very intrigued with astrology and quite a good astrologer himself. He did not, however, have the training required to really delve into charts and make sense of them. That was my job.

Van believed, as I do, in the power of prayer. Very often, he would be in deep thought, praying to God. He attended mass regularly at the local Baptist Church and felt the sermon almost always had something to offer, especially if you look for it. "You have to have spirituality in religion in order for it to mean something," he would say.

On January 31st, 2012, at 10:37 pm, while praying, he told me he could literally feel his prayer being answered. He said the experience was extremely intense and overwhelming, and he wanted to understand the astrological influences at that time of day to see if he could read into the spiritual occurrence even further. Sometimes, we experience a moment with God that takes us by surprise and makes us realize his omnipresence. This was clearly one of those rapturous moments for Van.

I was more than happy to discuss such an all-consuming and enlightening topic. Little did he know that 13 months later, Van would meet his creator face to face. Something he never dreaded. He often said he was not afraid of death, and if anything, he welcomed it.

Chapter 63

The Auction

I n the later part of 2011, Van called and said one of his attorneys was going to set up a meeting with Christies, the famed auction house in New York City. Since Van owed this attorney a considerable amount of money, he suggested that Van auction off his many possessions. Van disliked the idea right from the start. I could hear in his voice how an auction of his belongings would pierce his soul. I was extremely concerned and felt Van's emotional pain. We had, sometimes daily, phone conversations on who should handle the publicity, when he should fly to New York City, when he should sign the contract, and when the auction house representatives should come and assess his possessions. We ended up dragging out every transaction to make sure we had the most optimal dates possible. I was determined to have the auction and especially Van benefit from our conscientious effort.

On February 21st at 4:35 pm in Fort Worth, Van signed the contract agreeing that Christie's, the prestigious auction house in New York City, would be allowed to auction off many of Van's belongings, including some of his most prized possessions. Although this was an opportunity to gain a more stable financial footing, Van was not happy about letting go of memories and memorabilia.

His attorney set up the arrangement and, to Van's surprise, charged him for the transaction. Since he was to receive a portion of the auction profits for legal fees, the extra charge, which wasn't cheap by any means, was disappointing. Van described how some people are all about money. Although some people think it was his lifestyle, in my opinion, owing money was the ultimate culprit that brought Van Cliburn down. You would think that living in the land of billionaires and giving his heart and soul to the world, someone besides his trustworthy assistant would have offered more of their support.

Signing the contract for Christie's was just the beginning of his stress. Next were several engagements that involved luncheons, dinners, private parties, and teas, which mostly took place in New York City. Twenty engagements and a trip to London for dinner and a luncheon, plus a couple of days of filming and some interviews, were totally exhausting for Van. He wanted it all to stop.

One evening, I told Van that his health was taking too much of a toll and he needed to see a doctor. I was extremely concerned and actually upset at how he was being used. I was surprised at how so few came to his rescue.

Many beautiful and precious items were auctioned off. Van Cliburn was a collector of rare pieces of art and antiques from places all over the world. There was one painting in particular with an unusual Russian name, which would have had its home in a museum, that was given to Van by Shostakovich. Certain persons encouraged him to include it with the other auction pieces, but Van hesitated as he felt it would be an insult to Russia. The CEO head of Christie's agreed. Van was to keep the special work of art which Russia had intended for him to have.

The auction took place on May 17th 2012, in New York City. This date was part of a three-day window of auspicious astrological aspects that we aimed toward to make the auction a success. I remember sending Van a quick note saying, "Try to enjoy the Mercury/Jupiter aspect. I'm sure everything will be fine."

During this auction period, I was on the phone with Van every night. I was as reassuring as possible. It seemed like losing some of his precious belongings was just killing him. I could feel and hear his pain. I continued to encourage him to set up a doctor's appointment. His emotional health was destroying his physical health. Thus, he was clearly suffering. Van wanted to wait and thus finally saw a physician on July 22nd, 2013. The auction, however, was a total success, which I knew would happen, but it did little to relieve

Van of his daunting stress. The debilitating influences were now upon him.

Van was more concerned about the fact he was having trouble speaking as his voice had become rough, and his throat seemed very uncomfortable. Although he did see a physician about the roughness in his throat, this would gradually fade and be a minor issue in comparison to what Van was soon to encounter.

I was visiting my family in California and about to embark on a dining reunion on a warm summer day in July when I received a phone call from Van that would change my life once again. Van had bluntly received a death sentence from a Dallas Hospital! I was in absolute shock, but I also knew that he was deteriorating from the surmounting stress from the auction, along with earlier signs that his health was in a debilitating state. A great sadness filled me.

The realization of losing Van in my life when we still had so much more to explore in his lifetime was devastating. The thought of what he was going through was even more devastating. I collected myself and started working with Van on what would be one of our greatest ventures, prolonging his life.

We discussed every option and the timing of pursuing every treatment. The work was extremely involved, both mathematically and emotionally. The next step of treatment was constantly on my mind. I remained optimistic right up to our very last phone session.

Chapter 64

China's Invitation

A few days after the successful auction in New York City, a fax came in on May 22nd 2012, from China requesting that Van Cliburn perform a concert there. Van was very concerned and called me that evening. We thoroughly discussed how to address this request since Van believed in God and felt he could not play a concert for a communist country whose government consistently violated human rights. He was adamant about it!

It was obvious that the Chinese government wanted to use Van Cliburn's name, his worldwide status, and his contribution to classical music to enhance their own standing in the world when it came to classical music. Van did not like the idea of being used in this manner, nor did he believe in the policies of the Chinese government.

As Van felt it would be an engagement he would have trouble getting out of, he raised his price. China insisted on offering him any price! That's right, any price to perform a concert in mainland China. They wanted his name and status.

We were both quite surprised. Van would stick to his values and not sell out. Van stalled, and on July

22nd, after my prompting him for months to have his health checked, Van was diagnosed with terminal cancer. And that was his answer to China.

Chapter 65

Last Public Appearance

After Van adjusted to his new stark reality, we spoke more often about how he should plan the rest of his life. I knew from his astrology that it was going to be a socially busy cycle for the next five months, and it was. Whether it be connecting with doctors, supporting his foundation, or visiting with friends, there was much to do. Besides battling cancer, he was already scheduled to give a speech for the 50th Anniversary Gold Medalist Concert. Another MRI on August 12th 2012, continued to expose the obvious: Van Cliburn's life was coming to a close.

On September 6, 2012, at 7:30 pm at the Texas Christian University, Van Cliburn spoke for 3 minutes in honor of the Van Cliburn Foundation's 50th Anniversary Gold Medalist's Concert at Bass Performance Hall. It would be his last formal public appearance. Prior to the event, we carefully went over every aspect of his speech. Although well-prepared, he was terribly nervous. We discussed what he would say in length.

Van was reminded that evening by famed actress Greer Garson, best known for her role in Mrs. Miniver, who was a good friend of his. Ms. Garson wanted to enhance education and donated millions of dollars to

141

Texas Christian University. Van was present when she passed away in April of 1996 in Dallas, Texas.

Van Cliburn was questioning his own longevity, yet felt that passing away at the age of 78 was apropos of the incredible life he had lived. For the next six months, I inspired him as much as I could. He wanted to continue to live his full life, and even though he was fatally ill, he made a tremendous effort to attend many social functions that crossed his path during this short period. Attending dinners, many social engagements, a wedding, and allowing several people to visit him during a 6-month period before passing away kept him busy. He told me he never wanted to be a burden to anyone. However, I could feel, with each phone call, his life force slipping away. I remained optimistic regardless of the emotional pain that swirled around me.

I remember getting off the phone one evening and wondering how much more I could give to him, but I knew I must be there for him every step of the way, and I was.

Chapter 66

Chemo

For those of you who have experienced chemotherapy, you know what kind of courage and determination one has to have to even get through the treatments. Van and I were on the phone constantly trying to find the most optimal days to start and continue receiving the series of chemo. I kept hope alive with every session. The chemo treatments started on September 12th at 8:00 am. There was a series of six treatments and then a pause to see how the body was handling the dose given.

For the first four months, Van tolerated the chemo treatments quite well. In fact, he wasn't feeling any pain or illness. It was unusual and amazing. I was relieved. We continued to look for the best days and times to administer further treatments and get blood tests. However, I could see what was ahead, and so could Van. He would persistently question me on the very difficult astrological transits approaching in January and especially February of 2013.

One evening, Van expressed to me, "Between you, me, and the lamppost, I am leery of the other doctor I have." One of his doctors wanted Van to do radiation treatments after expressing how three of his patients had had it done. Van replied asking, "And did any of them live to tell about it?" There was no response, only an exchange of eyes that let the doctor know Van wasn't interested in being an experiment. As Van really didn't trust anyone, "Between you, me, and the lamppost" was one of Van's favorite lines.

Chapter 67

Final Days

I n life, we experience the heights and the depths. I embraced both experiences in my rapport with Van Cliburn. Hearing that his time on earth was very limited shook the core of my being. It was not supposed to be written in our script, but it was. Because of my responsibilities with my medically special needs child, we agreed to a time that we would speak that no longer possessed the lively spontaneity of the past that we were both so accustomed to in our elaborate sessions. And just about every evening at that time, Van would call. Although my new reality was devastating, my only consoling thought was the fact that Van Cliburn never seemed to fear death.

There was one thing I could count on when conversing with Van. He was always funny. He possessed a marvelous sense of humor that was so natural. Even in his dismal moments fighting cancer, you would think it didn't even exist by the way he was carrying on with his life. He even joked about his hair loss toward the end of his chemo treatments and how he had to wear a baseball cap so others visiting him would not be so shocked! Most everyone was used to his very full and handsome head of hair.

Still, there were times during this rough period when Van called me almost every night, hanging on to his last hope. Although concerned about the future, he accepted his fate gracefully.

In February of 2013, the last month of Van's celebrated life, I was speaking to Van about all of the stress he had been under recently. With despair in his voice, Van replied, saying, "Oh honey, you will never know." On so many levels, Van was holding up the world. I was always impressed. However, as an astrologer tends to keep their personal life out of the discussion, at that time, Van had no idea what I was going through in my life, nor did I want him to know the details. Serious health concerns, and my raising a medically special needs child, although a wonderful blessing, was all very challenging. I know my stress did not equal his, but it was still a ferocious force in my life. However, I was much younger and motivated toward healing. Van's health was slowly defeating him. His sense of humor was his shield. Always funny, right up to the last day I spoke with him before he passed away.

Chapter 68

A Child

I will never forget the two beautiful flower arrangements that Van Cliburn and Van's assistant had sent wishing my daughter and me well upon our return to the United States in September of 2009. I had been out of the country for almost two months trying to adopt her. It was an incredible journey that almost fell through at the last moment. Somehow, luck was on my side. Van called me a few times in Pavlodar, Kazakhstan, but did not want to bother me too much.

As my child grew into a beautiful little girl, she started demanding more of my attention. Van had to be a little more flexible with my schedule. Still, I made every effort to be there. Luckily, since most of our sessions were late at night, I could accommodate him.

Around October 2012, Van requested to see a photo of my daughter. He reminded me what an intense experience raising her was for me and that he was happy everything worked out.

I expedited a 5x7 inch photo in a frame to Van. After he had received it, Van started saying to me at the end of our sessions, "Now be sure to give your little one a kiss goodnight." I appreciated his words, as I tried not to dwell on the fact that one of our phone sessions was going to be the last. And then it happened. In my final conversation with Van on February 15th 2013, after going over some important topics, his last words to me were, "I want you to promise me that you will give your daughter a goodnight kiss." I said, I will. And his response was, "Christine, I want you to be sure and give her a goodnight kiss." Van knew his time was running out, and he was turning my attention to my daughter.

I remember Van thanking me for being there for him, saying, "You have no idea how much our sessions have meant to me." I replied, "I am always here for you, Van." It would be the last time I spoke with Van Cliburn.

Chapter 69

The Crossover

O n February 17th, Van was to have an intimate gathering for dinner with Angie Dickinson, Van's assistant, and Van's attorney. After discussing this date two days earlier, I specifically mentioned to Van that he should leave early and retire if he found his energy to be lapsing. I heard that he thoroughly entertained his guests and exhausted himself. The next day, Van started crossing over into the spiritual world, speaking to those who had already passed on. Ten days later, on February 27th at 9:40 am in Fort Worth, Van Cliburn took his final breath, allowing his soul to be released from his body.

Van's devoted assistant called me to personally tell me that Van had passed away. We had a very lengthy conversation. There was great sadness. He mentioned when the funeral would be. I called him back later, and we made arrangements for my arrival in Fort Worth, Texas. When I told him I could make it to the funeral, he said, "Van is smiling! You were a very important part of Van's life."

Chapter 70

Rachmaninoff's Romeo and Juliet

G oing back in time, when I returned from a trip in the summer of 2003, Van was right on cue with his call as he was always insightfully aware of when I was away. In asking me where I had been, I casually told him, with my strong ballet background, that I was on tour as stage manager for the Yellowstone Ballet production of Romeo and Juliet of the Rockies. The moment I mentioned that most of the music used was from Rachmaninoff, Van stopped me and said, "Don't tell me. Let me hum for you the music of the balcony scene," which Rudolph Nureyev and Margot Fonteyn are so famous for interpreting. I was in awe as he hummed with his deep, rich voice the adagio in Rachmaninoff's Symphony #2 in E minor, the exact music that was used for the famous balcony scene!

Since Van raved about Rachmaninoff, his absolute idol, I promised Van I would send him a DVD of the ballet to Rachmaninoff's music. Within the week it arrived, and Van called me after viewing and enjoying the entire performance. As my sister, Kathleen Rakela, had choreographed the ballet, he said, "Tell your sister, bravo, bravo, bravo!" For he knew that choreographing the ballet to Rachmaninoff's music was quite a feat.

Ten years later, I was sitting in a Baptist church in Fort Worth, crying my heart out at Van Cliburn's Funeral on March 3, 2013. When I finally collected myself, I turned the page and surprisingly noticed in the program the music, Adagio of Symphony #2 in E minor by Rachmaninoff. It was too good to be true!

When the Fort Worth Symphony started reverently performing the music for Van Cliburn, I could feel Van's presence humming and conducting the entire orchestra just ás he would have wanted. In the background, I visualized the balcony scene pas de deux of Romeo and Juliet. I was in heaven, and so was Van! The sounds that emanated from the symphony that day filled the church and sent us into rapture. The Glory of God was everywhere! Sometimes in life, you experience a perfect moment - this was one of them.

Van could not have been happier to have his favorite piece of music by Rachmaninoff, sending him off to his spiritual sojourn. For now, he is free to perform, conduct, write, or be what he wants to be in spirit. I'm glad he's happy now!

Chapter 71

After the Funeral

As I slowly exited the Baptist church, I watched as the hearse turned the corner, heading ever-so-slowly down the tree-lined street, and I said goodbye to Van, not wanting to look away. Taking a deep breath, I reluctantly looked the other way, and there stood the two people who had introduced me to Van Cliburn. I spent the rest of the evening with them. They expressed their thoughts to me, "Thank you for taking care of Van all of these years." It was my pleasure.

Chapter 72

Birthday Greetings

O n a rainy December day in 2012, Van mentioned that he had left a birthday message for me. Since it was left on a rarely used answering machine, it slipped my attention. He was so gracious about reminding me.

Later that evening, after speaking with Van, I heard the most beautiful birthday greeting, wishing me all good things for a prosperous new year. At the end of the message, he says, "I'll call you tomorrow. Have a good night, darling."

Upon returning from Van's funeral in Fort Worth, Texas, I happened to check this rarely-used voice messaging system, and lo and behold, there was the voice of Van wishing me a happy birthday, the only message still on there. It was a harsh realization to face the fact that I would no longer hear his deep, luscious voice ever again.

Chapter 73

Afterthoughts

In guiding Van Cliburn, I was always so in the moment that I had never thought about how it would feel when the moment wasn't there. Time seemed to stop. Everything in my life took on a whole new meaning. At times, I would freeze as the emotional sadness seemed to overwhelm me.

Van was unmistakably one of the peaks of my life at that time. Everything that I had worked so hard to achieve and attract this legend into my life seemed to be over. I wasn't sure where to go from here until the day I came home from Van Cliburn's funeral, and I sat down at my dining room table and started writing about the experiences I had shared with Van. It felt like he was right there with me, conversing once again, as I kept writing and writing. I started realizing I wanted to keep Van Cliburn alive.

This would be quite a task, but at least through Van's music, I was able to recreate his presence. It was in the autumn of 2000, during a session with Van, he suddenly said, "Do you have a copy of my DVD?" "No," I replied. "I will send you one." In a few days, the DVD, along with a CD that included some of the best collections of Van Cliburn's work, arrived in the mail. That evening, I watched and listened to what I will call the absolute brilliance of Van Cliburn. Today, it is my prized possession. For many days following his death, I put on Van's CD or DVD. Although emotionally sensitized, it helped me get through his absence at the time that we would speak, usually in the evening.

One afternoon, while driving in my car, I turned on the radio and heard the most beautiful piano playing emanating from the speakers. I commented to myself, saying, it's so good. It sounds like how Van Cliburn would have played. Sure enough, it was Brahm's Rhapsody No. 1 in B Flat by Van Cliburn. I took a pause in this lucid moment.

I was very affected by Van Cliburn's passing. It was a difficult reality to believe that I would never speak to him again. I had no one I could discuss these experiences with, and I felt so alone with my thoughts and memories.

Chapter 74

Looking Back

A bout a year and a half before Van passed away, he said he didn't miss playing the piano any more. Without the tremendous stress involved for him in performing a concert, I am sure it was a relief on many levels when he stopped. It wasn't just the playing of the piano, but it was the position in life that he held. In some ways, he was holding up the world with his genius, warmth, incredible talent, hospitality, and barrier-breaking ways. He was a truly wonderful human being, a man unparalleled in the world today. We are all fortunate to have had him grace our planet when he did.

Chapter 75

Game Shows

Walking into Van Cliburn's home on the day of his funeral, I felt his presence everywhere, especially near all of the framed photos that had claimed their space on his grand piano. Van's personal assistant showed me a blackboard with "Van Cliburn" written out, which brought a smile that held memories. His signature was reminiscent of the very popular show, What's My Line, that Van was featured on as a mystery guest. During a phone consultation, Van had told me that he had such fun fooling the panel and audience, pretending to be someone other than himself by applying a well-practiced Russian accent to all of his answers. I was reminded of how Van thoroughly enjoyed the television show Jeopardy, the cerebral king of game shows that he watched frequently.

One Friday evening in July of 2013, approximately four months after Van passed away, I was pleased to hear that the clue in the final round of Jeopardy was: The cover of the May 19, 1958 Time Magazine called him, "The Texan who conquered Russia." The answer: "Who is Van Cliburn?" Now you know. Van Cliburn was even more than an outstanding legendary pianist and crusader for classical music, but a true messenger who brought culture, enlightenment, and peace to the world.

THE END

My writing this memoir is to remember an incredible man on so many levels that I and millions loved and admired. I was honored to guide him. I hope I have shown you what a phenomenal artist and friend Mr. Cliburn was and how he truly believed that classical music was the real prize and he wanted everyone to experience it.

Van and I greatly respected one another, but our goal was the music. He said, "Civility and cultivation breed better music." Being that he found a way into the forefront of my life, I was always concerned about Van. I often wished that I didn't have to charge him for our sessions as I thoroughly enjoyed his company and many stories. However, from Van's perspective, when you pay for something, you want it to have value. With his collection of fine art, he understood the word "value".

Van always practiced the piano late at night after our sessions. Practicing for hours and hours pushes one into the etheric world of music. One can't help, but become more sensitive to humanity. Van's spiritual side would gradually develop, and he would come to not question experiences that were considered otherworldly. "One evening, when my mother was sound asleep. I awakened to hear, Rildia Bee, Rildia

Bee! It was my grandmother calling out my mother's name, I will never forget it."

Van's spirituality would go further in exploring the world of astrology. During our time together, he was brilliantly able to incorporate astrology not only into his life, but also while performing Haydn, Chopin, Rachmaninoff, Liszt, and Brahms, amongst others.

There is one astrological point that needs to be told. Van Cliburn was born on July 12, 1934, in Shreveport, Louisiana. Van's Jupiter in his astrology chart was exactly conjunct to the USA Saturn at 14 degrees Libra, where Jupiter alleviates the restrictions of Saturn and enhances solid, expansive potential. This enabled Van to do something for the United States that would reinstate its desired, worldly status. His Jupiter also favorably aspected Putin's Sun, and Putin's Jupiter favorably aspected his Sun exactly, which encouraged a positive rapport between them.

Whether it be for artistic or political reasons, Putin was very congenial to Van. Unfortunately, he does not share that same concern for a neighboring country.

Van was appalled by the atrocities that go on in this world, and I felt, at times, that he looked forward to his spiritual sojourn. On January 23, 2008, at 1:26 am, Van humorously said to me, "I will not call you again tonight unless I die, and then I will just come and say bye-bye!" We both laughed, not knowing this was a premonition of the future. I have yet to be visited by Van, but I have heard from a heavenly soul that he is performing concerts in heaven and loving it!

The Messenger

In New York City, after winning the Gold Medal, Van Cliburn gave a speech that far exceeded his years as a young man, telling the audience how he was not only honored to be the winner of the First Tchaikovsky Competition, but also that he was only a messenger and a witness to his garnished talent from God. Van Cliburn often spoke of how he was a messenger of classical music, and he lived out that theme for the rest of his days, never wanting to steal the spotlight away from the prize of classical music.

The Honors

V an Cliburn was awarded the Charles E. Lutton Man of Music Award in 1962, and he was honored at the Kennedy Center Honors on December 2, 2001. Van Cliburn received the Presidential Medal of Freedom on July 23, 2003, from George W. Bush, the Grammy Lifetime Achievement Award in 2004, and on September 20, 2004, the Order of Friendship from President Vladimir Putin. He also received the National Medal of Art from President Obama on March 2, 2011. Van Cliburn has performed for most president from Harry S. Truman to Barack Obama.

Christine Rakela

The Dream

O n June 21st, 2015, I had a vivid dream concerning Van Cliburn. I suddenly realized I was in an extremely large theatre which was off-white, shaped in an oval, and completely open on one side where I was standing near several small café-like tables with chairs, staring at a well-dressed elite audience gazing sadly at the stage. Their profiles said it all and were undisturbed. All of a sudden, I was startled by Van's presence everywhere. I had entered a memorial for Van Cliburn!

From the stage, a mixture of jazz and classical music emanated that seemed all wrong in describing Van Cliburn. My first thought was the audience was not hearing what Van Cliburn wanted them to hear. No one really knows who Van is. To the left of me, out of the corner of my eye, I noticed two people, a young man and a woman, who were looking at me. I glanced in their direction. The young lady smiled. Her familiar face put me at ease. I realized I was fashionably dressed in a black outfit with a white robe that seemed inappropriate and was quickly discarded on a nearby chair. I took one last look at the audience and what they were missing, and then I awoke. This dream only further confirmed for me the need to tell Van's story.

Glossary

Acapella: Music that is performed without instrumental accompaniment by a singer or a group

Acoustics: The sound that emanates from a musician, speaker, or singer as it reverberates within a room, theatre, auditorium, etc.

Astrology: The study of the stars, including the planets, zodiac signs, and house sectors that helps us understand the past, deal with the present, and offer guidance into the future,

Bass Performing Hall: A performing arts center in Fort Worth, Texas.

Beethoven, Ludwig Van: An admired German composer and pianist who excelled during the Classical Period. His music compositions are some of the most performed works. Although he became deaf, he continued to expand upon his innovative works.

Brahms: A German composer and pianist who wrote during the Romantic Period symphonies, concerti, chamber music, and choral compositions.

Bruno, Walter: A German pianist, conductor, and composer known for his Viennese interpretations. He escaped Nazi Germany in 1933 and settled in the United States conducting for the Metropolitan Opera.

Bush, George W.: An American politician who was the 43rd president of the United States from 2001 to 2009.

Callas, Maria: An American-born Greek soprano who was one of the greatest opera singers. Her rise to fame was due to her dramatic interpretations, her bel canto technique, and her wide-range vocals.

Carnegie Hall: One of the most prestigious music halls on 57th Street in Manhattan that was built by Andrew Carnegie, who garnered millions during the Industrial Age.

Christie's Auction House: A high-class auction house established in 1776. It was founded by James Christie, has worldwide access, and yearly accrues billions of dollars in sales.

Chopin, Frederick: A Polish composer who was also a piano virtuoso who wrote solely for the piano during the Romantic Period. He maintains worldwide recognition for his poetic style in music.

Classical Period: An era where classical music was expanded upon, thus gaining popularity around 1750 to 1820, which was between the Baroque and Romantic Periods.

Cliburn, Harvey Laven: Van Cliburn's father who was an oil industry executive in Texas for Exxon Mobile.

Cliburn, Rildia Bee O'Bryan: Van Cliburn's mother who was a musician, pianist, and teacher. She studied under Arthur Friedheim in hopes of becoming a concert pianist. She also ran a riverside mission in Shreveport, Louisiana.

Cold War: An extremely intense rivalry that existed between the United States and the Soviet Union, where there was no military engagement between 1945 and 1991.

Communism: A far-left economic and political ideology that pertains to socialism, which exercises control over one's freedoms so that all people experience sameness.

Competition: Two or more persons or groups vying for the same prize that leads to a winner. A competition garners a winner and a loser.

Concerto: An instrumental composition that was established in the Baroque period, written for one or more soloists who were featured with an orchestra or ensemble group.

Costa, Mary: An American film actress and singer, who also sang opera and was a soprano opera star.

Dickinson, Angie: An exceptional American film and television actress. She is mostly known for her role in the television series, Police Woman. She has also appeared in many movies.

Evans, Linda: An American actress who excelled in her roles on television and gained tremendous popularity. She is mostly recognized in the dramatic series called Dynasty. She also appeared in several movies.

Fontayn, Margot: An English ballerina who became a principal dancer with the Royal Ballet and received world recognition when performing with her renowned dance partner Rudolph Nureyev.

Garland, Judy: An American actress, singer, and dancer who also did vaudeville. Although she played many different roles during her career, she is known for her portrayal of Dorothy in The Wizard of Oz.

Grand Staff: A staff which is composed of two different staves used in music, a treble staff and a bass staff. Using the grand staff, one is able to notate music for instruments of both low and high pitches.

Greer Garson: An American actress and singer who gained popularity during WW11 through Metro-Goldwyn Studios.

Gold Medalist: Medals that are awarded to the winner who has shown excellence in a competition or sports game.

Gorbachev, Mikhail: One of the last Russian leaders of the Soviet Union until 1991. He also held the position of General Secretary of the Communist Party.

Although a Marxist/Leninist, he moved the country toward a social democracy.

Harpsichord: A musical instrument that relies on a keyboard to be played. The harpsichord may have more than one keyboard and a pedal. It was used in Renaissance and Baroque music and gradually disappeared when the piano became popular.

Haydn, Franz Joseph: An Austrian composer who lived during the Classical Period and is noted as one of the most prolific composers. Haydn's collection included 107 sympathies, 83 string quartets, 45 piano trios, 62 piano sonatas, 14 masses, and 26 operas.

Honorary Doctorate Degree: An honorary degree awarded by a university to someone who has met the merits' of excellence in their chosen field, where the specific requirements are waived.

Horn, Lena: An American singer, actress, and dancer who was also an activist for human rights. She appeared in film, theatre, and television for over 70 years.

Jeopardy: Popular cerebral king of game shows that quizzes its contestants by giving roundabout answers to questions that need to be answered.

Johnson, Lyndon B.: An American politician who was the 36th president of the United States from 1963 to 1969.

Julliard: One of the most prestigious schools specializing in music, dance, and drama. It is the oldest and largest school located in New York City. It offers undergraduate and non-artistic degrees and specializes in musical training.

Jupiter: It is the 5th planet from the Sun and also the largest in our solar system. In astrology, it represents good fortune, opportunity, expansion, and optimism.

Kabuki: The intense, stylized, classical performance in Japanese theatre that encompasses elaborate traditional dance with drama.

Kennedy, John F.: An American politician who was the 35th president of the United States from 1960 to 1963. He was assassinated in November of 1963.

Kremlin, The: A fortified complex that lies in the center of the city of Moscow. It is composed of five palaces and four cathedrals and is surrounded by the Kremlin wall and towers. It is also the residence of the Russian president.

Khrushchev, Nikita: A Soviet Union politician who held the office of First Secretary of the Communist Party for 11 years and Chairman of the Council of Ministers for 6 years. He denounced Stalin and pursued a policy of destalinization.

Liszt, Franz: A Hungarian composer in the 1800's who was also a conductor, piano virtuoso, and teacher during the Romantic period. He became popular over the course of six decades of diverse classical works.

Lunar Return: An astrology chart that is based on the Moon returning to its natal position as a transit that foretells trends for that particular month.

Mallay, Edna St. Vincent: An American poet, playwright, and feminist in the Roaring Twenties. She won a Pulitzer Prize in 1923 and also the Frost Medal for poetry.

Medal of Valor: The highest awarded military medal for bravery.

Metronome: A small device that has a regular interval, audible sound used for keeping a distinctive pace with the music being played or sung.

Mercury: The second smallest planet in our solar system, when Pluto is considered, and the closest planet to the Sun. In astrology, it is the planet of communication, learning, writing, and local travel.

Mitropoulos, Dmitri: A Greek composer, conductor, and pianist who started his career at a very early age. He did not use a baton and sometimes conducted from the keyboard from memory. He directed the Athens Conservatory, the Minneapolis Symphony, the New York Philharmonic, the Metropolitan Opera, and the Orchestra of La Scala.

Moscow: Standing near the Moskva River, Moscow is the largest city and the capital of Russia. In the city limits, its population is 13 million.

Mozart, Wolfgang Amadeus: One of the most influential composers during the Classical period. His prolific talent created over 600 music compositions. He started composing music at the age of five.

National Endowment: An independent agency that offers funding as well as support for outstanding artistic projects and works with the United States federal government.

Neptune: Known as the eighth planet in our solar system. In astrology, it rules over illusion, vague deception, and dissolvement in adverse aspect and creativity and spirituality when in positive aspect.

Nureyev, Rudolph: One of the greatest male ballet dancers and choreographers from the Soviet Union. He achieved fame when he defected from the Kirov Ballet in 1961 and joined the Royal Ballet and their lead dancer, Margot Fonteyn.

Olga Kern: A Russian-born, American classical pianist who rose to fame at the Van Cliburn International Piano Competition in 2001.

Plato: An ancient Greek philosopher who was born in Athens. Plato founded a school of philosophy called The Academy.

Price, Leontyne: The first African-American soprano who was acknowledged internationally and was affiliated with the Metropolitan Opera House as their lead opera singer.

Prokofiev, Sergei: A highly regarded Russian composer, conductor, and pianist who created masterpiece compositions across different music genre lines.

Putin, Vladimir: The President of Russia since 2012. He has also served as the minister of Russia since 1991 and, prior to that, was the first Deputy Chairman of St. Petersburg. He was also an intelligence official.

Queen Elizabeth: The longest reigning Monarch, Queen of the United Kingdom and the Commonwealth for 70 years and seven months until her death in 2022.

RCA: The Radio Corporation of America was an innovative company founded in 1919 and reigned over the electronics and communications industry for five decades. Van Cliburn was signed exclusively to RCA.

Rachmaninoff, Sergei Vasilyevich: A brilliant Russian composer, pianist, and conductor who was known for his virtuoso piano performances of romanticism in classical music. In his compositions, the piano is prominently featured. Rachmaninoff was Van Cliburn's exceptional idol.

Reagan, Ronald W.: An American actor and politician who was the 40th president of the United States from 1981 to 1989.

Rice, Condoleezza: She is the first black woman to serve as national security advisor and Secretary of State. She is a political scientist, educator, and American diplomat and is the director of the Hoover Institution at Stanford University. She is also an accomplished concert pianist.

Romantic Period: An artistic movement that started in Europe between 1800 and 1850, where intelligence persuaded artistic expansion. Romanticism was also a movement that emphasized individualism, enlightenment, and emotion.

Rostropovich, Olga: Artistic Director of Mstislav Rostropovich International Festival and the Galina Vishnevskaya Opera Centre in Moscow. Daughter of cellist and conductor Mstislav Rostropovich and singer Galina Vishnevskaya

Saturn: The sixth planet in our solar system that astrologically implies hardship, challenges, and control.

Shostakovich, Dmitri: An acclaimed Soviet-era Russian pianist and composer who achieved fame with his first symphony in 1926. He was a noted panelist that judged Van Cliburn in 1958 when he won the gold medal.

Solar Return: An astrological chart that indicates a new yearly cycle as the Sun returns to its natal position when you were born.

Soviet Union: The Union of the Soviet Socialist Republic that was governed by communism from 1922 to 1991.

Sputnik 1: The first satellite launched by the Soviet Union that would encircle the Earth in an elliptical low orbit on October 4th, 1957. It was artificial and sent radio signals back to Earth for three weeks before its batteries died.

Steinway Pianos: One of the world's finest handcrafted piano companies for over 160 years. Van Cliburn endorsed and only played on Steinway pianos.

Stevens, Rise: An opera singer who was a mezzo-soprano and an American actress. She sang for the Metropolitan Opera House for two decades and is known for her portrayal of Carmen by Geoge Bizet.

Stokowski, Leopold: An American conductor that was strongly affiliated with the Philadelphia Orchestra and was the music director of the New York Philharmonic Symphony, Cincinnati Symphony Orchestra, NBC Symphony Orchestra, and Houston Symphony Orchestra.

Sun: The star in our solar system that the other planets orbit. A planet in astrology that represents the will, one's goals, vitality, recognition, and pride.

Sun Line: Refers to the aspect the Sun is making to a particular point in the astrology chart, thus influencing that sector. Achievement and recognition are experienced under a Sun line aspect. Also, in astro-cartography and local space, the imaginary line that the Sun affects around the globe from an astrological perspective.

Tchaikovsky, Peter: A remarkable Russian composer who achieved international fame during the Romantic Period and wrote operas, ballets, concertos, and symphonies, which left a lasting impression. He composed his first song at the age of four.

Tebaldi, Renata: A popular Italian Lirico-spinto soprano who performed at La Scala and Metropolitan Opera Houses during the post-war period.

Tithing: The practice of giving a portion of your income (usually 10%) to charity or religious organizations.

Van Cliburn International Competition: An American piano competition established by Van Cliburn in 1962 in Fort Worth, Texas, that is held every four years and is the most recognized competition in the world.

What's My Line: A game show where a panel of four guests ask a contestant questions, who is hidden backstage to determine who he is.

Zodiac: Twelve different horoscope signs, each displaying their strengths and weaknesses according to what constellation element they reside in.

In "My Private Relationship with Van Cliburn" by Christine Rakela, discover the captivating journey of Van Cliburn, a classical music prodigy who changed history. As one of the most trusted people in his life, the author's personal relationship with Cliburn led her to write about his fascinating life stories, often using his own words. The book offers an intimate look at the man behind the piano, one of the greatest pianists in history, and how Cliburn took his talent to new heights never experienced before. Although rocketing to superstardom, behind the scenes, he encountered jealousy and loss, yet great love from others.

The book's narrative reveals the personal struggles and triumphs of a musical genius, showcasing Cliburn's wisdom and his lasting legacy. Christine Rakela's personal account, as his advisor, invites readers to embrace the inspiring, meaningful, and sometimes riveting story of Van Cliburn's life. Keeping to his vision of enlightening the world, Cliburn's passion for classical music was a destiny that drove his soul.

About the Author

Christine Rakela is an internationally known astrologer who is certified through the National Council for Geocosmic Research. She has had a full-time practice for over 30 years. Christine has produced and hosted an independent television program, "Astrology Connection," in New York City to a wide audience for 22 years. She has also been a featured guest on national television and radio, lectures throughout the country, and has written several articles for two different magazines. Christine is the published author of three books. She resides in the Greater New York Area.

Made in the USA
Las Vegas, NV
19 April 2024

88770656R00105